Table of Contents

I. Introduction

China's extraordinary rise to global prominence over the last quarter century raises significant strategic military questions for the United States. The size of China's military and its impressive force modernization programs have enhanced the capabilities of a once regionally focused power. As China's requirements for strategic resources expand with its growing economy, it continues to come into competition and friction with states and transnational entities outside of its traditional spheres of influence. Although economic partnerships and diplomatic initiatives between the United States and China have made violent military conflict between the two less likely, China's growing global strategic interests necessitate greater military force projection capabilities that have begun to put it in competition with those of the United States and its North Atlantic Treaty Organization (NATO) allies. The U.S. National Security Strategy of 2006 and Quadrennial Defense Review of 2010 acknowledge China's increasingly global orientation, expressing concern for the uncertainty of its strategic military intentions.[1] Two important and interrelated military strategic questions arise from this uncertainty: How can the United States confront and overcome military threats from China, should they arise? Does China have a discernable way of war against which the U.S. military and government can plan, prepare, and adapt?

The Science of Military Strategy, an important strategic military text published in 2001 by the Chinese Academy of Military Science, provides an insightful examination of contemporary Chinese military strategy. According to this study, the first and most important tenet of China's strategic guidance, paraphrased from the writings of Mao Zedong, is "You fight in your way and *we fight in ours*, and strive for full initiative.[2] Describing the significance of this core strategic principle, the authors state,

---

[1] Office of the President of the United States of America, *The National Security Strategy of the United States of America,* (March 2006), 41 and Department of Defense, *Quadrennial Defense Review,* (Feb 2010), 31.

[2] Peng Guangqian and Yao Youzhi, eds., *The Science of Military Strategy*, (Beijing: Military Science Publishing House, 2005), 452. Italics inserted by author for emphasis. The more common spelling of Zedong is the Wade-Giles Romanization, "Tse-Tung."

"This principle is the soul and quintessence of strategic guidance of China and the Chinese Army. It is the most precise and vivid theoretical condensation for the guiding law of the people's war and the supreme realm in guidance for war throughout war history. It has distinct Chinese characteristics and the spirit of times."[3] This key tenet of China's strategic guidance implies the existence of a Chinese "way" of war that is different from other ways of war. However, the qualities, characteristics, and origins of this unique Chinese way of war are generally unknown to most modern Western military audiences.

While Western scholars have provided a rich body of literature describing how Western societies including the United States wage war, they have offered little similar analysis of Chinese warfare. The theory of the "Western way of war," promoted principally by Victor Davis Hanson in his works *Carnage and Culture* and *The Western Way of War* and extended by other notable scholars, such as John Keegan and Geoffrey Parker, provides an approach to understanding the patterns of warfare of a civilization by analyzing the historical and cultural influences that make it distinctive from other ways of war. Other influential books such as Robert Citino's *The German Way of War,* Russell Weigley's *The American Way of War*, and Archer Jones's *The Art of War in the Western World* also present theories that describe the unique characteristics, trends, and preferences of particular states or civilizations in the art and science of waging war.

Western scholars, such as Keegan, have made some attempts at describing an "Oriental" way of war juxtaposed to the Western, but there is a dearth of English language literature that attempts to determine the existence of a Chinese way of war.[4] John Lynn explains this scarcity in broad analyses of Chinese warfighting writing that "Arguments that there were no real non-Western parallels for Western military practices result all too much from our ignorance of non-Western warfare…We know more about ancient China, but that understanding does not rival our command of Greek and Roman military

---

[3] *Ibid.*

[4] John A. Lynn, *Battle: A History of Combat and Culture from Ancient Greece to Modern America,* (Philadelphia: Westview Press, 2003), 19.

history."[5] David Graff provides further explanation arguing that "in contrast [to scholarship in Chinese], relatively little work on Chinese military history has been published in English and other Western languages…For the most part, the ideas of innovative Western military historians, from Hans Delbruck to John Keegan and Martin van Creveld, have yet to be applied to the study of Chinese warfare."[6] While there are many exceptional English language works on China's military history, few, if any, attempt to synthesize a unified theory about Chinese warfare in the tradition of Western scholars such as Hanson, Citino, Keegan, and others.

This study attempts to narrow this gap in our understanding of Chinese warfare throughout history by providing a study that answers the question "Is there a Chinese way of war?" It addresses other broad exploratory questions including the following: What are the general characteristics and propensities of Chinese warfare and how do they compare to those of the West? What are the continuities in Chinese warfare throughout its long military history? Finally, what are the cultural, philosophical, and historical influences that have shaped Chinese warfare? The ultimate goal of this research is to broaden our understanding of Chinese warfare throughout history and to inform U.S. military strategists and professionals about some of the strategic implications of the Chinese way of war.[7]

Understanding the Chinese way of war is important to the U.S. military for several reasons. American military professionals can learn much from the rich martial history of China, which in return, can help broaden their appreciation for non-Western warfare. Additionally, the perceivable future will likely involve greater interaction between American and Chinese military forces. Therefore, a better

---

[5] *Ibid.*

[6] David A. Graff and Robin Higham, eds., *A Military History of China,* (Boulder: Westview Press, 2002), 17.

[7] Note on spelling: This monograph uses the Hanyu Pinyin spellings for Chinese words and names as it is now the standard recognized by the People's Republic of China and the International Organization for Standardization. Pinyin is the most recent Romanization of the Mandarin language, based on the phonetic pronunciation of its words, and provides the approved modern spellings for Mandarin Chinese using the Roman alphabet.

understanding of Chinese culture and military traditions will help to more effectively shape future operations, partnerships, exchanges, and other forms of dialog and interaction. The study of military arts and sciences in the classrooms of the U.S. military's academic institutions, such as those of the U.S. Army's Command and General Staff College, almost exclusively focuses on of warfare in the West. Throughout their military education, American officers learn in great detail about the histories of the wars in Europe, the campaigns of the American Civil War, the organization and structure of the German General Staff, the Western way of war, and Allied combined arms during the wars of the twentieth century. They also study at length the military philosophies of Clausewitz, Jomini, and other influential Western strategists. While the typical mid-grade American officer possesses adequate applicable knowledge of Napoleon, Grant, Frederick the Great, Eisenhower, or Rommel, he or she is likely to know little of the great Chinese military leaders and philosophers save Mao Zedong or Sunzi.[8] This disparity highlights a major weakness in the military education of U.S. officers, which could be significantly improved with a more balanced focus on the history of warfare outside beyond that of Western states.

Nearly absent in this education is an understanding or appreciation of warfare by non-Western states and civilizations. The service paid to Chinese warfare and military philosophy in the U.S. military is often cursory and insubstantial. Randomly inserted into military field manuals, publications, and briefings are quotes from Sunzi and Mao Zedong that lack context, explanation, or substantive interpretation. Yet historical texts of Chinese warfare in the English language reveal an excellent military tradition full of case studies and relevant examples of important military topics and considerations such as leadership, grand strategy, organizational theory, operational art, tactics, maneuver, and planning. Considering the importance of China's role in contemporary world events and its several centuries of military history, it becomes clear that the education of US military officers would greatly benefit from a deeper and broader understanding of the Chinese way of war. Contemporary US counterinsurgency

---

[8] Sunzi is better known under the Wade-Giles Romanization, "Sun Tzu."

operations have sparked a new interest in the theories and writings of Mao Zedong, but beyond that little or no additional study of Chinese warfare occurs in the military education of American officers. Although the United States military has firmly established itself as the premier state military in the world today, it can still greatly learn, develop, and improve from a balanced study of the warfighting styles and strategies of other states, such as China.

A. Thesis

Three and a half millennia of Chinese civilization have indeed produced a distinctive and enduring Chinese way of war. While the art and science of war in China have evolved considerably, the characteristics and philosophies of its style of warfare contain some *propensities* that endure from antiquity to the present, which include the following: The Chinese military orientation focuses more on the strategic and operational levels of war than the tactical. The Chinese prefer strategic maneuver warfare to attritional or other forms of warfare. Chinese warfare emphasizes the importance of shaping operations, the arrangement of the conditions of the war, campaign, or battlefield in one's favor before initiating combat. Finally, deception and unorthodox warfare play a leading role in Chinese warfare.

These four themes of the Chinese way of war are best described as propensities, since thirty-five hundred years of Chinese military history naturally contain some outlying examples of warfare waged differently during certain events or eras. The four propensities are *general trends* that emerge when the entire span of Chinese warfare is broadly considered. They were developed during China's ancient era in the philosophy of the great military scholars and on the battlefields of the Warring States and early Imperial eras. These traditions have endured through many centuries of Chinese military history and continue to exist today in the Chinese Peoples' Liberation Army (PLA). When considered individually, some of the four propensities may not be exclusive to Chinese warfighting alone. For example, China is not unique in its preference for maneuver warfare or its emphasis on the use of deception in combat.

However, when aggregated the four propensities create a way of war that is unique to Chinese military history and philosophy.

The Chinese way of war is a reflection of the distinctive cultural, religious, and philosophical traditions of China's long and extraordinary history. It provides continuity in the military customs and philosophies of the ancient warring armies of the pre-imperial kingdoms and the modern forces of today's PLA. A deeper understanding of China's warfighting propensities can help to shape and inform more effective U.S. military strategy towards China. Additionally, the military forces of the United States and its Western allies can learn much from the unique practices of Chinese armies throughout history and the martial philosophies of the great Chinese strategists. A study of Chinese warfare can also better inform our understanding of Chinese culture, politics, and history as that nation takes a more prominent role in contemporary world events. One of the most influential American Sinologists, John K. Fairbank, emphasized the importance and enduring value of this understanding. "Study of the Chinese way in warfare can ease the rest of the world's necessary adjustment to China's participation in the new transnational order," he believed. "Thus an understanding of China's military tradition has practical value: not only to help us deal with its inheritors in Peking but also to help us ourselves inherit its virtues and eschew its evils. China's history is now part of our general inheritance."[9]

Suggesting that a way of war exists in China does not imply that Chinese warfare is in any way stagnant or incapable of change and adaptation. China is not trapped in the military customs and martial patterns of the past. On the contrary, Chinese military traditions have evolved tremendously over the last three thousand years and continue to do so today. The history of warfare in China is as colorful and variable as that of any other state or civilization. Just as with the evolution of today's PLA, armies throughout China's history have been capable of innovation and progress. Yet even with change and

---

[9] John K. Fairbank, "Introduction: Varieties of the Chinese Military Experience," *Chinese Ways in Warfare,* Frank Kierman and John Fairbank, eds., (Cambridge: Harvard University Press, 1974), 2.

evolution certain propensities and tendencies still emerge to make Chinese warfare unique and continuous. These propensities form the basis for the Chinese way of war and are an inheritance of the proud military traditions of this ancient civilization.

B. Methodology

This study begins by detailing a theory of the Chinese war of war, which links Chinese military philosophy from the ancient to modern eras and describes the propensities that make this style of warfare unique to the Chinese civilization. The next segment describes Chinese warfare during military campaigns in three different eras and analyzes the validity of the theory. This section examines a major military operation in each era that is representative of the general warfighting characteristics of that time. It begins with an analysis of ancient Chinese warfare during the late Han Dynasty, with the Red Cliffs Campaign (208-209 CE) as the centerpiece of the study. The research continues with an examination of medieval Chinese warfare during the Tang Dynasty, focusing on the Pamirs Expedition and the Battle of Talas (747-751 CE). The final case study provides an analysis of modern Chinese warfighting, centered on China's First and Second Phase Offensives of 1950 during the Korean War.

Each case study attempts to draw some of the links between war, philosophy, and culture that defined and evolved the Chinese style of war during these eras and describes continuities in Chinese warfare between the three. This study does not take into consideration attributes such as courage or leadership, which are universal human qualities, nor does it compare levels of discipline and esprit de corps, which are hallmarks of any good military organization, regardless of culture. Each of three campaigns contains significant military operations that accurately portray the techniques, characteristics, methods, and philosophy of Chinese warfare that existed during their eras. These case studies focus at the campaign level order to capture the characteristics of warfare at the operational and strategic levels of war rather than the tactical. The study concludes with recommendations for further areas of study and provides policy and doctrine implications for U.S. strategic decision makers and military professionals.

II. A Theory of the Chinese Way of War

A. Introduction

The Chinese way of war has four propensities that tend to distinguish it from the warfighting preferences of other civilizations: 1) Influenced heavily by the writings of the classic strategists of ancient China, the military orientation of the Chinese way of war focuses more on the strategic and operational levels of war than the tactical. 2) The Chinese prefer strategic maneuver warfare to attritional or other forms of warfare. 3) Chinese warfare emphasizes the importance of shaping operations, the arrangement of the conditions of the war, campaign, or battlefield in one's favor before initiating combat. 4) Deception and unorthodox warfare play a leading role in Chinese martial philosophy and conduct of war. These characteristics of the Chinese way of war pervade China's long military history and may be found in the texts of its great military philosophers and in accounts of warfare from antiquity to the present. These propensities are influenced by thirty-five centuries of Chinese cultural ontology and are deeply influenced by the social, religious, and philosophical underpinnings of the civilization.

As a generalization of Chinese warfare over the past three millennia, Chinese military strategy and philosophy tend to emphasize the strategic and operational levels of war more than the tactical. The strategic level of war orients on the state and its national military objectives and strategies. At this level, the rulers of the state and its highest-ranking military leaders develop and enact plans and policies to achieve long-term strategic objectives by leveraging the state's resources and instruments of power.[10] The operational level of war consists of the employment of military forces in major operations and campaigns to achieve strategic objectives. The tactical level of war involves the use of combat power in engagements and battles. This is the level in which adversary combatants clash in battle, and it is most

---

[10] The U.S. Army's *Field Manual 3-0: Operations* defines the strategic level of war as "the level of war at which a nation, often as a member of a group of nations, determines national or multinational (alliance or coalition) strategic security objectives and guidance, and develops and uses national resources to achieve these objectives." See *FM 3-0*, page 6-2.

concerned with the short-term employment of forces in relation to each other on the battlefield.[11] Engagements and battles at the tactical level are strung together into campaigns and major operations at the operational level, which, in turn, win wars and achieve national objectives at the strategic level. The Chinese way of war deemphasizes the importance of fighting and winning individual battles in favor of an orientation towards the strategic and operational objectives of war. While the texts of classic Chinese military philosophy contain a great deal of guidance on the tactical employment of forces, the greatest Chinese strategists and generals considered the tactical level of war to be the least important and most simple aspect of warfare. Indeed, the greatest of all Chinese military theorists, Sunzi, stated emphatically, "For to win one hundred victories in one hundred battles is not the acme of skill. To subdue the enemy without fighting is the acme of skill. Thus, what is of supreme importance in war is to attack the enemy's strategy."[12]

Unlike the art of war in the West, the Chinese prefer strategic maneuver warfare to attritional or other forms of warfare. Strategic maneuver warfare in this sense refers to the use of operational and strategic maneuver to achieve strategic objectives, while attritional warfare refers to the use of a state's strategic resources to achieve strategic objectives. Critics may argue that warfare in the West, especially in the modern era, also focuses on maneuver to win wars. However, when one considers from a strategic perspective the major wars of the twentieth century, such as the two World Wars, it becomes clear that these were ultimately contests of attrition.[13] The Allies defeated Germany and Japan in World War Two by using their superior resources over time to drain the enemy's manpower, resources, and will to fight. As a broad generalization, Chinese warfare throughout the ages has been focused more on the strategic positioning and employment of forces to win wars rather than on overwhelming

---

[11] *FM 3-0,* page 6-3.

[12] Sunzi, *The Art of War*, Samuel B. Griffith trans. (Oxford: Oxford University Press, 1963), 77.

[13] The same argument can be applied to the Allies victory over the Central Powers in the First World War. After four years of stalemate, the strategic resources of the Allies outlasted their adversaries', enabling final victory.

adversaries through the expenditure of superior strategic resources. This concept of wielding and employing a force's strategic disposition of power, "*shi,*" is central to Chinese military theory and practice.

Chinese warfare places great emphasis on the arrangement of the conditions of a war, campaign, or battlefield in one's favor before initiating combat, a process that modern American strategists refer to as "shaping operations."[14] The true test of a Chinese military commander is not in the actions taken or decisions made during a battle but before it. A skillful general in the Chinese cultural ontology only embarks on a campaign or takes the field of battle once he has shaped conditions in his favor. He selects when and where to fight and forces the enemy to move in reaction to his behavior. "It is a doctrine of war," claimed Sunzi, "not to assume the enemy will not come, but rather to rely on one's readiness to meet him; to not presume he will not attack, but rather to make oneself invincible."[15] Therefore, the ancient Chinese approach considers those decisions and preparations that an army makes before combat at any level of war, such as the positioning of forces, arrangement of logistics, establishment of alliances, reconnaissance, and selection of terrain, to be more important and more difficult than actions taken during the actual fighting. To the Chinese a critical aspect of shaping operations is strategic patience. A skilled general waits until all of the most favorable conditions are set before he takes violent action. Another important element of Chinese shaping operations is to force one's adversary to move or to act in ways that are advantageous to oneself. Genius in Chinese warfare is not moving to the enemy, but making the enemy move to where you want him to move.

The fourth propensity of the Chinese way of war is the importance placed on the use of deception in warfare. This propensity underlies a fundamental difference between Chinese and Western views of war. The Chinese have no reservations on the use of deception in battle, while practitioners of

---

[14] The U.S. Army's *Field Manual 1-02 Operational Terms and Graphics* defines shaping operations as "operations at any echelon that create and preserve conditions for decisive operations." *FM 1-02*, page 1-170.

[15] Sunzi, 114.

the Western way of war, as a generality, view deception as inferior to other principles of war, such as massing one's forces at the decisive point of a battle. One of the most influential modern Western military theorists, Antoine Henri Jomini, made almost no mention of deception in his landmark study of warfare, *The Art of War*. Believing that surprise and deception were almost impossible to achieve in modern combat, Jomini placed the focus of his theories on overt tactics in battle, writing:

> Before the invention of fire-arms surprises were more easily effected than at present, for the reports of artillery and musketry are heard for so great a distance that the surprise of an army is now *next to impossible* unless the first duties of field service are forgotten and the enemy is in the midst of the army before his presence is known because there are no outposts to give the alarm. [16]

In contrast, the Chinese display no reticence towards the use of deception and consider it to be a critical element of combat. In one of his most famous stratagems, Sunzi stated, "All war is based on deception. Therefore, when capable, feign incapacity; when active, inactivity...Attack where he is unprepared; sally out when he does not expect you. These are the strategist's keys to victory."[17]

B. The Four Propensities in Chinese Military Philosophy

The four propensities of the Chinese way of war can be found in many of the writings of both ancient and modern military philosophers from Sunzi to Mao Zedong. They are recurring themes in the military classics of ancient China and can be found in Chinese military texts throughout the ages. These characteristics emerge again and again in the classic literature and are echoed by subsequent Chinese military philosophies.

---

[16] Antoine Henri Jomini, *The Art of War*, J.D. Hittle, ed., *Roots of Strategy Book 2: du Pic's Battle Studies, Clausewitz's Principles of War, and Jomini's Art of War*, (Mechanicsburg: Stackpole Books, 1987), 513. Italics inserted by author for emphasis.

[17] Sunzi, 66-70.

1. Orientation at the Strategic and Operational Levels of War

Sunzi and the ancient strategists believed that victory in war necessitated a broad strategic approach that focused all of the efforts of the military to achieve the objectives of the state. "War is a matter of vital importance to the state; the province of life and death; the road to survival and ruin," wrote Sunzi in the opening passage of *The Art of War*.[18] Beginning his treatise with this statement, Sunzi established the primacy of the strategic level of war and the subordination of military objectives beneath the strategic political objectives of the state. In Sunzi's view the ultimate goal of war is for a state to achieve its political objectives with military force as quickly as possible and with the least cost to the state. Since war is the "road to survival and ruin for a state," it must be fought in a way that minimizes risk to one's own state while increasing risk to the enemy's state.[19] Sunzi wrote:

> What is essential in war is victory, not prolonged operations. And therefore the general who understands war is the Minister of the people's fate and the arbiter of a nation's destiny...
> Generally in war the best policy is to take a state intact; to ruin it is inferior to this. To capture the enemy's army is better than to destroy it; to take intact a battalion, a company, or a five-man squad is better than to destroy them...Your aim must be to take All-under-Heaven intact. Thus your troops are not worn out and your gains will be complete. This is the art of offensive strategy.[20]

The classic scholars believed that to achieve this kind of rapid, total victory, the military commander must not focus on the individual tactics of battlefield combat but on the strategic framework of the war and issues regarding the war as a whole. Commanding generals in war must allow their subordinate leaders to handle the tactics, while they focus on the strategic outlook and resolve the strategic problems of the war. All actions in combat, regardless of whether they are at the tactical, operational, or strategic levels of war, must be synchronized and directed towards supporting the achievement of strategic objectives. To the classic theorists, military commanders erred when they focused on fighting over strategy.

---

[18] Sunzi, 63.

[19] Edward O'Dowd and Arthur Waldron, "Sun Tzu for Strategists," *Contemporary Strategy*, (Vol 10, January 1991), 28.

[20] Sunzi, 76-77.

While the classic texts of Chinese military philosophy deal largely with tactical considerations such as types and employments of unit formations, the use of combined arms, combat leadership, and battlefield maneuvers, an overarching theme throughout the writings of Chinese strategists is the paramount importance of orientation towards an entire war rather than individual battles and victories. As in the ancient Chinese board game *weiqi*, which has influenced Asian culture and military thought for centuries and is still popular today, overall strategy is more important than tactics.[21] [See Appendix 1, Figure 1] The skilled *weiqi* player looks beyond tactical considerations on any part of the board and considers the overall strategic arrangement of stones across the entire board and over the total duration of the game. The game of *weiqi* provides an accurate metaphor for the Chinese orientation at the strategic and operational levels of war. The game, which requires the capturing of an opponent's stones to win, necessitates a kind of *grande strategy* that transcends small victories in favor of strategic advantages. Those experienced in the game become willing to sacrifice stones when doing so accords with their overall strategy. Novices of *weiqi* focus on the act of capturing stones, and this tactical orientation prevents effective deliberation on the broader strategic considerations of the game.

As in *weiqi*, Chinese warfare and military philosophy deemphasizes the accumulation of tactical victories to achieve strategic objectives in favor of a strategic outlook and a holistic approach to waging war. The Chinese way of war acknowledges the overarching requirement for superior strategy rather than superior tactics in war. An army that is victorious in a hundred battles will ultimately lose the war if it focuses on winning battles without a strategic thread to bind them together.[22] This thought is echoed in the writings of the great Chinese general and strategist Wuzi (440 to 361 BCE), who stated:

---

[21] *Weiqi's* traditional Romanization is *"wei ch'i."* It is also called *go* or *igo* in Japan and *badu* in Korea, this two-player board game originated in China some three thousand years ago. Today, *Weiqi* is still played by millions of people worldwide. Played on a wooden grid, this game of strategy requires contestants to capture their opponent's white or black stones. See American Go Association, http://www.usgo.org/resources/whatisgo.html.

[22] An historical example of this phenomenon includes the United States defeat in the Vietnam War, in which the United States outfought the North Vietnamese in nearly every battle and major engagement but ultimately lost the war.

Now being victorious in battle is easy, but preserving the results of victory is difficult. It is said that among the states under Heaven that engage in warfare, those that garner five victories will meet with disaster; those with four victories will be exhausted; those with three victories will become hegemons; those with two victories will be kings; and those with one victory will become emperors. For this reason those who have conquered the world through numerous victories are extremely rare, those who thereby perished are many.[23]

Wuzi and Sunzi share a similar strategic orientation that cautions against the deceptive nature of tactical success. True skill entails decisive victory through planning, conditions setting, positioning, and maneuver that are guided by a holistic overarching strategy. The classic Chinese military texts also speak of the related concept of *quan*, the strategic balance of power, and concern for this element of warfighting is the hallmark of military greatness. In the Chinese military ontology, tactics are easy and require little with respect to genius and wisdom. The maintenance of strategic objectives and the effective wielding of strategic power, however, are the pinnacle of generalship in the Chinese way of war. The *Ssu-ma Fa,* an influential forth century BCE military text, introduces the concept of wielding strategic power. "In general, warfare is a question of the strategic balance of power [*quan*], and combat is a matter of courage."[24] In his writings about China's revolutionary war nearly 2,400 years later, Mao Zedong echoed this philosophy, explaining that the orientation of his protracted war must be strategic, not tactical in nature. Mao wrote:

> Why is it necessary for the commander of a campaign or a tactical operation to understand the laws of strategy to some degree? Because an understanding of the whole facilitates handling of the part, and because the part is subordinate to the whole. The view that strategic victory is determined by tactical success alone is wrong because it overlooks the fact that victory or defeat in war is first and foremost a question of whether the situation as a whole and its various stages are properly taken into account. If there are serious defects or mistakes in taking the situation as a whole and its various stages into account, the war is sure to be lost.[25]

---

[23] Sawyer, *The Seven Classics of Ancient China,* 208.

[24] *Ibid,* 134.

[25] Mao Zedong, "Strategy in China's Revolutionary War," *The Evolution of Military Thought: Selected Writings of Mao Tse-Tung,* (Ft. Leavenworth, Combat Studies Institute), 81-82.

Heavily influenced by Sunzi and other classic philosophers, Mao understood that his Red Army could not achieve ultimate victory against the Guomindang (GMD or Nationalists) through tactical success. Throughout his writings Mao continued to emphasize the strategic nature of the conflict, arguing that the Red Army itself played a critical strategic role, serving "as an armed body for carrying out the political tasks" of the overarching strategy of the war.[26] Mao described the indelible tie between political power and the military. In his view military power enabled the achievement of political objectives. This thought was evident in one of his most famous maxims, "Political power grows out of the barrel of a gun…whoever has an army has power, for war settles everything." Mao's emphasis on the strategic and operational levels of war provides a clear linkage of this important propensity in Chinese military philosophy from the ancient to modern eras.

2. Strategic Maneuver Warfare

Warfare in the Chinese tradition hinges on the concept of strategic maneuver. Strategic maneuver is the artful movement and positioning of forces and available resources to enable strategic positional advantages against one's adversary. A metaphor that recurs in the ancient texts likens the maneuver of an army to the flowing of water. In this comparison the philosophical and cultural influences of Daoism on Chinese warfighting become apparent. One of the central principles of Daoism is the concept of *wu wei,* a notion that nature must be allowed to follow its course as a river flows to the sea. *Wu wei* is a belief in natural action or "effortless doing" that has deeply influenced Chinese culture and philosophy. Applied to the art of war, *wu wei* and the water analogy depict the manner in which an army must maneuver during a campaign or on the field of battle. Sunzi embraced this metaphor, writing:

---

[26] *Ibid,* 54.

Now an army must be likened to water, for just as flowing water avoids the heights and hastens to the lowlands, so an army avoids strengths and strikes weaknesses. And as water shapes its flow in accordance with the ground, so an army manages its victory in accordance with the situation of the enemy.[27]

The water metaphor implies that strategic maneuver must be in harmony with the terrain, the weather, and the enemy situation. Armies must maneuver in a manner consistent with their nature and with the characteristics of the environment. This philosophy contrasts with the Western value of individualism, which suggests that man determines his own destiny, and his will is greater than nature.[28] Western culture values the individual spirit and power of human will to accomplish the extraordinary. In this ontology mankind can shape the world through the force of his will and is constrained only by the scope of his imagination and the depth of this commitment.[29] The philosophical underpinnings of Daoism, however, restrain mankind to act in concert with the laws of nature. Applied to Chinese warfare, the concept of *wu wei* provides a powerful metaphor for tactical and operational maneuver. A skillful general must not force his army to move in ways that are disharmonious with its nature, the terrain, and its positional relationship with the enemy. It is "the Way of unimpeded harmony" as described in the Dao De Jing that the victorious commander applies to the art of maneuver warfare.[30] In doing so, the commander capitalizes on the inherent potential of his force and the terrain and maximizes his chances for victory. As suggested in the *Wei Liaozi*, an influential fourth century BCE military text, "The Army that

---

[27] Sunzi, 101.

[28] The conquests of Alexander the Great and Napoleon Bonaparte provide excellent examples of this central notion of Western philosophy. Western culture values the individual spirit and power of human will over nature. In this ontology mankind can shape the world through the force of his will and is constrained only by the scope of his imagination and the depth of this commitment.

[29] Francois Jullien explains the philosophical roots of this Western mindset, claiming, "Greek philosophy trains Western thought to set up an ideal form (*eidios*), which we take to be a goal (*telos*), and then we act in such a way to make it fact. It all seems to go without saying- a goal, an ideal, and will: with our eyes fixed on the model that we have conceived, which we project on the world and on which we base a plan to be executed, we choose to intervene in the world and give form a reality." See Francois Jullien, *A Treatise on Efficacy: Between Western and Chinese Thinking,* (Honolulu: University of Hawaii Press, 2004), 1.

[30] Thomas Cleary, trans., *The Essential Tao: An Initiation into the Heart of Taoism Through the Authentic Tao Te Ching and the Inner Teachings of Chuang Tzu,* (New York: Castle Books, 1992), 10.

would be victorious is like water. Now water is the softest and weakest of things, but whatever it collides with- such as hills and mounds- will be collapsed by it for no other reason than its nature is concentrated and its attack is totally committed."[31] Here, the *Wei Liaozi* embraced the Daoist notion that force is inferior to non-force. "What is softest in the world," suggested Laozi[32], "drives what is hardest in the world."[33] In this sense, a skilled commander achieves victory not merely through the application of force but through capitalizing on the potential of the situation and the nature of the circumstances in the war.

The Chinese tradition views strategic maneuver warfare as a superior method to achieve victory in war. Attritional warfare, waged so expertly by the states and armies of the West, is somewhat antithetical to Chinese culture and philosophy. A skilled general does not force victory through the sheer expenditure of men and resources but through an exploitation of the opportunities inherent in the situation and environment. *The Methods of the Sima* explained the essence of strategic maneuver in warfare:

> Determine the [number of] your masses in accord with the terrain, and deploy your formations in accord with the enemy. When attacking, waging battle, defending, advancing, retreating, and stopping, the front and rear are ordered and the chariots and infantry move in concord, this is termed a well planned campaign…Being able to be large or small or firm or weak, to change formations, and to use large numbers or small groups- all in respects being a match [for the enemy]- is referred to as 'exploiting the balance of power' [*quan*] in warfare.[34]

According to the classic theories, a skilled commander fully understands his army, his enemy, the terrain, and all elements of the environment and from this wisdom is able to determine the best and most responsible employment of his force. He does not force victory by simply overpowering his enemy with superior numbers and weapons, as is the general strategy in attritional warfare. In strategic maneuver warfare, a commander strives to preserve his own resources, use the terrain and the situation to his advantage, and when possible to take his enemy intact. "What is essential in war is victory, not prolonged

---

[31] Sawyer, *The Seven Military Classics of Ancient China*, 257.

[32] Laozi, author of the *Dao De Jing* and founder of Daoism, is better known by the Wade-Giles Romanization, "Lao Tzu."

[33] Cleary, 35.

[34] Sawyer, *The Seven Military Classics of Ancient China*, 135.

operations," stated Sunzi.[35] Once again, the game of *weiqi* provides an accurate metaphor for Chinese warfare. In the game, the number of stones that a player has in play is much less important than the strategic configuration of his stones on the board. Through strategic maneuver, the emplacement of stones in accordance with one's overall strategy, a player can make his opponent conform to his strategy and control the flow and tempo of the game. Through strategic maneuver a skilled *weiqi* player controls the flow of the game, uncovers subtle opportunities, and capitalizes on advantages that become inherent over the course of the game.

Strategic maneuver implies not only movement on the part of an army but also movement and actions that force the enemy into modes of reaction. The consequence of skillful strategic maneuver is that one's adversary is forced to act outside of his original strategy. In Sunzi's view "Those skilled at making the enemy move do so by creating a situation to which he must conform. They entice him with something he is certain to take, and with lures of ostensible profit they await him in strength."[36] Through strategic maneuver a general can dictate the course of a battle or campaign by forcing his adversary to unknowingly conform to his strategy through direct and indirect movement, deception, and diversion. Sunzi stated "When I wish to give battle, my enemy, even though protected by high walls and deep moats, cannot help but engage me, for I attack a position he must succor. When I wish to avoid battle I may defend myself simply by drawing a line on the ground; the enemy will be unable to attack me because I divert him from going where he wishes."[37] In this way, a successful commander takes control of events and circumstances on the battlefield, turns them in his favor, and forces his adversary into an unprofitable paradigm of reaction and countermeasure.

---

[35] Sunzi, 76.

[36] Sunzi, 93.

[37] *Ibid*, 97.

18

Mao applied the concept of strategic maneuver warfare to his campaigns against the Guomindang in a strategy he called "mobile warfare."[38] Juxtaposed to positional warfare used by the Soviet Union or attritional warfare waged by the GMD against the Red Army, Mao based his theory of mobile warfare on the concept of fluidity, echoing the ancient Daoist metaphor of water and Sunzi's de-emphasis of tactical success.[39] This fluidity was physical, regarding the transience of his battle lines and the mobility of the Red Army, and also psychological, regarding adaptive thinking and flexibility in the minds of his officers. Mao wrote:

> In a revolutionary civil war, there cannot be fixed battle lines…Fluidity of battle lines leads to fluidity in the size of our base areas. Our base areas are constantly expanding and contracting, and often as one base area falls another rises. This fluidity of territory is entirely a result of the fluidity of the war…We generally spend more time in moving than in fighting and would be doing well if we fought an average of one sizable battle a month. 'Fight when you can win, move away when you can't win.'—this is the popular way of describing our mobile warfare today. All our 'moving' is for the purpose of 'fighting,' and all our strategy and tactics are built on 'fighting.'[40]

Again, Mao's application of classic military philosophy provides continuity in the warfighting propensities of the ancient and modern Chinese worlds. Like Sunzi, he viewed the art of strategic maneuver warfare as one of the most difficult and important concepts to master when commanding forces in war. When applied correctly, strategic maneuver can provide an inferior force the means to defeat a vastly superior adversary. Mao's victory over the Nationalists was due to his brilliant application of mobile warfare, his rejection of attritional warfare, and his overarching focus on the war from a strategic perspective. [41]

---

[38] The Guomindang is better known by the Wade-Giles Romanization, "Kuomintang" or KMT.

[39] Mao Zedong, 146.

[40] *Ibid*, 138-130.

[41] Mao believed that attritional warfare was inferior to maneuver warfare and would also be a poor strategy for his force considering its numerical and material inferiority to the armies of the Guomindang. "It is inappropriate to advocate a 'contest of attrition' for the Chinese Red Army today," he claimed. "'A contest of treasures' not between Dragon Kings but between a Dragon Kings and a beggar would be rather ludicrous." See Mao Zedong, "On Protracted War," 146.

3. Shaping Operations

Chinese warfare emphasizes the importance of shaping operations, the arrangement of the conditions of the war, campaign, or battlefield in one's favor before initiating combat. Sunzi stressed the importance of pre-battle calculations and preparations in warfare. He believed that a good commander first estimates the enemy's position and strength against his own and determines his relative advantages. He creates advantageous conditions, waits for favorable opportunities to arise, and only then chooses to engage or withdraw. He sets the conditions of the battle, campaign, or war in his favor before initiating combat. "Therefore he who is skilled in battle establishes himself in a position where he cannot be defeated, and does not let slip [the opportunity] to defeat the enemy," he believed. "For this reason the victorious army first conquers and only then seeks to fight."[42] Termed "shaping operations" by the U.S. military, these activities are "operations at any echelon that create and preserve conditions for the success of the decisive operation."[43] Sunzi encouraged military forces to take decisive action at the time and place of their own choosing, rather than the enemy's by shaping the conditions of war before taking the field. This is the positional advantage, mentioned by Sunzi, from which a commander "cannot be defeated." Once a military unit achieves this through shaping operations, it can strike an enemy decisively on preselected terrain and at a time of its own choosing.

What makes the Chinese emphasis on shaping operations distinct from the warfighting preferences of other states or civilizations is its belief that these pre-battle actions and condition-setting operations are *more important than the fighting itself.* "Those skilled in war subdue the enemy's army without battle," claimed Sunzi. "They capture his cities without assaulting them and overthrow his state

---

[42] Mark E. Lewis, *Sanctioned Violence in Early China*, (Albany: State University of New York Press, 1990), 116.

[43] Headquarters Department of the Army, *Field Manual 3-0: Operations*, (February 2008), 5-11.

without protracted operations.[44] Absent here are any Western notions of glory or honor, the *doxa* (δόξα) that Thucydides claimed every man desires, gained through heroic actions such as facing one's adversary in combat.[45] Deeply influenced by the Daoist notion of *wu wei*, which in this sense denotes "action by inaction" or "effortlessness," the ancient Chinese strategists including Sunzi viewed victory without struggle to be the epitome of military art.[46] Therefore, genius in warfare lay in the actions and preparations undertaken by a commander to achieve victory before battle and less so in the final clash of arms.

A critical aspect of Chinese shaping operations is patience at all levels of war. Setting the conditions of war in one's favor involves waiting until certain criteria are met and circumstances of the environment and the enemy become favorable. The commander must possess the wisdom and skill to strike only when the time and conditions support his force. Written five or six centuries before Sunzi's *Art of War,* T'ai Kung's *Six Secret Teachings* described strategic patience as essential to military excellence. According to T'ai Kung, "One who excels at warfare will await events in the situation without making any movement. When he sees he can be victorious, he will arise; if he sees he cannot be victorious, he will desist."[47] This rational approach to warfare is much more difficult in practice. The art of strategic patience is one of the most complex combat leadership skills to master. Indeed, the military histories of China and the West are replete with examples of armies defeated as a result of tactical impatience and failure to set favorable conditions before the initiation of combat.

---

[44] Sunzi, *The Art of War*, 79.

[45] Thucydides wrote that man is primarily motivated by three factors: fear (*phobos*), greed or self-interest (*aplistia*), and honor or glory (*doxa*), and he believed that all wars are fought for these reasons. See Robert Strassler, ed., *The Landmark Thucydides: A Comprehensive Guide to the Peloponnesian War,* (New York: Touchstone, 1996), Book I, Chapter 3.

[46] John K. Fairbank, *China a New History,* (Cambridge: Harvard University Press, 1992), 54.

[47] Ralph Sawyer, trans., *The Seven Military Classics of Ancient China,* 69.

Shaping operations in the Chinese military tradition are tied directly to the concepts of vulnerability and invincibility. A skilled practitioner takes the field of battle only after he has done what is necessary to make himself invulnerable to the enemy.[48] This invulnerability stems from creating advantages that are positional, numerical, logistical, technological, and/or moral in nature. Once invulnerability is established, the general simply waits for the enemy's moment of vulnerability and attacks.[49] Shaping operations enable a commander to dictate the pace, rhythm, and timeline of a battle or campaign. He determines when and where fighting will take place and under what conditions. His adversary is thereby compelled into a mode of reaction rather than action. Through shaping operations, the commander controls the critical elements of combat and forces his enemy to move and to act on his terms. Rather than moving to the enemy, a skilled commander compels the enemy to move to him. As described by Sunzi, "Generally, he who occupies the field of battle first and awaits his enemy is at ease; he who comes later to the scene and rushes into the fight is weary. And therefore those skilled in war bring the enemy to the field of battle and are not brought there by him."[50]

Mao made exceptional use of shaping operations to achieve his strategic objectives during China's' protracted war of resistance against the Japanese military from 1937 to 1945.[51] Indeed, he wrote that the stages of the protracted war were but conditions-setting operations to enable the final counter-offensive against the Japanese. Mao did not view any phase to be more important than the others, since each required the setting of critical conditions and no phase could be initiated without the completion of these strategic shaping operations. He believed that the Chinese forces must shape the conditions of the

---

[48] Although true invincibility can never be achieved in combat, one can apply the figurative meaning of Sunzi's stratagem, which connotes taking precautions to guard against defeat by strengthening weaknesses and protecting vulnerabilities.

[49] Sunzi stated, "Anciently the skillful warriors first made themselves invincible then awaited the enemy's moment of vulnerability." See Sawyer, *The Seven Military Classics,* 85.

[50] Sunzi, 96.

[51] Also called the "Second Sino-Japanese War."

war in stages in order to achieve victory. Mao's focus on the criticality of shaping operations in this strategic outlook during the war with Japan reveals a consistency in the Chinese way of war that had been carried from ancient times to the modern era.

4. Deception and Unorthodox Warfare

Unlike the Western way of war that orients on direct, overt confrontation in combat, the Chinese way of war places great emphasis on the art of deception. In the West, deception is considered useful but not necessary to warfare. Western military philosophy focuses on the direct approach to warfare, while Chinese philosophy encourages the use of direct and indirect approaches together to achieve the best effects in combat. Sunzi insisted that "He who knows the art of the direct and the indirect approach will be victorious." In contrast, Western military philosophers such as Jomini and Clausewitz orient almost exclusively on directness of action in combat rather than the indirectness of deception and trickery. *On War*, Clausewitz's seminal study of warfare, contained only the sparsest discussion of deception, which he termed "cunning."

> Strategy is exclusively concerned with engagements and with the directions relating to them…Analogous things in war- plans and orders issued for appearances only, false reports designed to confuse the enemy, etc.- have as a rule so little strategic value that they are used only if a ready-made opportunity presents itself…It is dangerous, in fact, to use substantial forces over any length of time merely to create an illusion; there is always the risk that nothing will be gained and that the troops deployed will not be available when they are really needed. In war generals are always mindful of this sobering truth, and thus tend to lose the urge to play with sly mobility. Stern necessity usually permeates direct action to such an extent that no room is left for such a game.[52]

In stark contrast to this is the Chinese orientation towards deception and its myriad uses in war. Not only is the use of deception a hallmark of effective Chinese warfare, it must be *central to the strategy of any combatant in war*. Since all war is based on deception, as Sunzi suggests, the art and the use of deception must be foundational to any war plans or stratagems. While deception in war is practiced by

---

[52] Clausewitz, *On War,* 202-203.

Western armies, it is generally done to a lesser degree or with less emphasis than by the Chinese. In Western military operations, the deception operation is rarely the main effort, although some historical outliers exist.[53] For the most part Western warfare focuses on direct, decisive action. The main effort must be, as Jomini states in his principles of war, "to throw by strategic movements the mass of an army, successively, upon the decisive points of a theater of war… and on the battlefield to throw the mass of the forces upon the decisive point, or upon that portion of the hostile line which it is of the first importance to overthrow."[54]

To the ancient Chinese war scholars "deception" included both the art of deceiving one's opponent and the use of "unorthodox" warfare, termed *qi*.[55] According to Sawyer this concept refers to employing methods that are "unusual, unexpected, marvelous, strange, heterodox, and sometimes eccentric." The art of *qi*, he explains, "involves creating and exploiting the tactical imbalances that enable its practitioners to achieve victory against vastly superior forces."[56] Again it is important to consider that Chinese military philosophy places no moral judgment on the ethics of deception in combat. It views deception and unorthodoxy in warfare from a pragmatic perspective and considers their artful use to be the acme of military strategy.

There is also a key psychological component to the art of deception in Chinese warfare. Graff explains the centrality of stratagems and psychological considerations in traditional Chinese military philosophy and practice. "Accounts of medieval Chinese battles are filled with ambushes, feigned flights, and all sorts of surprises, tricks, and traps," he claims. "This literature indicates that the goal of

---

[53] Examples of the use of deception in Western warfare at the operational and strategic levels of war include Washington's Christmas crossing of the Delaware in 1776, the German invasion of Western Europe in 1940, and the Allied invasion of Normandy in 1944.

[54] Jomini, 461.

[55] The more common spelling of this word is the Wade Giles Romanization, "ch'i."

[56] Ralph D. Sawyer, *The Tao of Deception: Unorthodox Warfare in Historic and Modern China,* (New York: Basic Books, 2007), 6-9.

commanders in battle was not simply to overpower their opponents, but somehow to achieve a psychological effect that would trigger the collapse and panic-stricken flight of the opposing army.[57] Sawyer also believes that this psychological manipulation of the enemy included "enervating the rested, destabilizing the composed, [and] stirring chaos in the well-ordered."[58] Sunzi explored the variations and employment of deception in war at length:

> When the enemy is at ease, be able to weary him; when well fed, to starve him; when at rest, to make him move. Appear at places to which he must hasten; move swiftly where he does not expect you...Therefore, against those skilled in attack, an enemy does not know where to defend; against the experts in defense, the enemy does not know where to attack. Subtle and insubstantial, the expert leaves no trace; divinely mysterious, he is inaudible. Thus he is the master of his enemy's fate.[59]

The ancient Chinese understood well how forms of deception and manipulation can imbalance one's adversary and wear away at his troops' morale. They have both a practical and a psychological effect on the balance of power on the field of battle and over the course of a campaign. Thus, deception acts as a critical enabler that can change the course of a war, even when one's opponent possesses superior numbers and capabilities. In modern terms, the Chinese view the art of deception and the use of unorthodox warfare as key combat multipliers.

Having built the philosophical foundation for the study, the following sections of this monograph explore the Chinese way of war in practice by analyzing military campaigns in China over three historical eras. These sections test the viability of the four propensities of Chinese warfare by confirming their existence, describing them in action, and exploring the continuity of these characteristics from antiquity to the present. The analysis of these campaigns also demonstrates the extent to which the practice of Chinese warfare matches its philosophical roots.

---

[57] David A. Graff, *Medieval Chinese Warfare, 300-900* (New York: Routledge, 2007), 168.

[58] Sawyer, *The Tao of Deception*, 70.

[59] Sunzi, 96-97.

III. Imperial Chinese Warfare: The Red Cliffs Campaign (208-209 CE)

A. Introduction

The Red Cliffs Campaign, 208-209 CE, was one of the most famous events in all of Chinese military history.[60] The story behind this extraordinary operation and the epic narrative that surrounds it has achieved a near mythical status in Chinese folk culture and literature. Featured prominently in one of the greatest literary classics of China, *Romance of the Three Kingdoms* by Luo Guanzhong, this campaign and its major military engagement, the Battle of Red Cliffs, contained all of the necessary elements for an enduring story that would inspire readers for centuries. Red Cliffs involved a historical backdrop ripe with political intrigue, displays of remarkable courage and leadership on both sides of the conflict, large-scale riverine naval warfare, and the employment of unorthodox tactics and methods. It is a classic tale of an underdog's triumph against overwhelming odds. Indeed, even today the characters and events of this remarkable battle continue to compel modern audiences.[61]

The Red Cliffs Campaign was emblematic of the military strategy and operational art of the late Han Dynasty period.[62] It showcased the best in combat innovations of the age, including advanced naval technology, devastating firepower through missile warfare, and complex operational maneuvers. In this campaign, imperial forces under Cao Cao faced off against a numerically inferior coalition of southern states along the banks of the Chang Jiang River in southeast China.[63] While the exact location of the campaign's final engagement, the Battle of Red Cliffs, remains an issue of some debate amongst scholars,

---

[60] Peter Lorge, "Water Forces and Naval Operations," *A Military History of China*, David Graff ed., 85.

[61] In November 2008, Hong Kong director John Woo released his two-part epic film "Red Cliffs" (*"Chi Bi,"* a fictional account of the Battle of Red Cliffs. The film was received by Chinese and international audiences with enormous box office success and critical acclaim including wining several international film awards. The film's theatrical release in the US was in November 2009.

[62] Also called *Chi Bi* and Red Cliff.

[63] The Chang Jiang River is the largest in Asia and is best known by the traditional Romanization, "Yangtze."

many believe that it occurred near the present day city of Wuhan in the Fujian Province.[64] The Red Cliffs

operation showcased the best of military art and science in China's Later Han Era.[65] Although many of

the key players and events of the fighting are clouded by centuries of Chinese romantic fiction and folk

legend, it is possible to discern the major actions that took place and construct a short, accurate account of

the fighting. Although only a snapshot in the long military history of China, the Red Cliffs Campaign

serves well to represent the methods, strategies, and art of war in late ancient China.

B. Historical Setting

The Red Cliffs Campaign occurred during an era in Chinese history known as the "Three

Kingdoms" period from 189-316 CE. Punctuated by the great collapse of the Han Empire, this was a time

of constant warfare and great political upheaval that became highly romanticized in Chinese literature as

an age of adventure and chivalry.[66] The four centuries of Han Dynasty rule prior to the Three Kingdoms

period were characterized by considerable population growth, increased domestic and foreign trade, and

military expansion. However, by the middle of the first century, Han control over China was in rapid

decline and nearing its total collapse. The fall of the dynasty may be attributed to a number of ailments,

most significantly the rise in power of regional authorities over the central government, weak imperial

leadership, external threats from adversaries along the frontiers, and disunity within the imperial court.[67]

By the Late Han, military power continued to be more greatly consolidated in the hands of regional

---

[64] Zhang Xiugui, "Ancient 'Red Cliffs' Battlefield: a Historical-Geographic Study," *Frontiers in the History of China*, Vol 1, Number 2, June 2006, 214.

[65] Rafe di Crespigny, "The Three Kingdoms and Western Jin: A History of China in the Third Century AD, Internet Edition 2003," Australian National University, http://www.anu.edu.au/asianstudies/decrespigny/3KWJin.html (accessed October 10, 2009).

[66] C.J. Peers, *Soldiers of the Dragon: Chinese Armies, 1500 BC-AD 1840,* (Oxford: Osprey Publishing Ltd., 2006), 78.

[67] John K. Fairbank, *China: A New History,* (Cambridge: Harvard University Press, 1992), 72.

warlords, rather than the imperial court.[68] A period of warlordism corresponded with the Han's decline as powerful regional leaders and autonomous kingdoms began to exert their influence in the power vacuum created by a growingly ineffectual central government. The strength and influence of warlords over the central government was solidified during the great rebellion of the Yellow Turbans in 184, when imperial leadership turned to warlord commanders to put down the uprising. These warlords, in turn, continued to form large, powerful armies loyal only to them.[69]

By the time of the Red Cliffs Campaign, what remained of the Han Empire was split amongst the three most powerful warlord kingdoms, Wei in the north, Shu in the Sichuan basin of the southwest, and Wu in the southeast, along the South China Sea. The period of the Three Kingdoms spanned the gap between the end of the Han Dynasty and the advent of the Jin Dynasty and was characterized by a half century of continuous civil war.[70] This era marked the longest period of violent conflict since the founding of the Han Dynasty in 206 BCE.[71] Each of the three kingdoms claimed legitimate rights to the Han imperial throne, but Wei in the north, seated in the imperial capital and situated at the heart of the state bureaucracy, wielded the greatest power.[72] Its leader, Cao Cao, a legendary statesman and general of Han China, sought to reunite the separate kingdoms of the former Han Empire, either through diplomacy or by force.[73]

---

[68] Edward Dreyer, "Continuity and Change," *A Military History of China,* David Graf and Robin Higham, eds., (Cambridge: Westview, 2002), 31.

[69] Rafe De Crespigny, "The Military Culture of Later Han," *Military Culture in Imperial China*, Nicola di Cosmo ed., (Cambridge: Harvard University Press, 2009), 110.

[70] Graff, *Medieval Chinese Warfare*, 18-19.

[71] *Ibid,* 18.

[72] Here "Wei" refers to what remained of the Eastern Han Empire in 208 CE. The name Wei was not actually assigned to the kingdom until five years after the events at Red Cliffs. For simplicity, this monograph uses the name "Wei" when referring to Cao Cao's forces.

[73] By the time of Red Cliffs, Cao Cao served in the positions of Chancellor and Commander-in-Chief of the Eastern Han Empire. Although his sovereign, the Emperor Xian, was technically still the ruling monarch of the dynasty, Cao Cao wielded the actual political power of the throne.

C. The Red Cliffs Campaign

1. The Campaign

By 207 CE, Cao Cao, arguably the greatest Chinese politician and military strategist of his day, controlled nearly half of China's territory and population, commanding the Wei kingdom in the north and bent on subjugation of the southern powers and reunification of the Han Empire. Having been victorious in central China and seeking to maintain the strategic initiative, Cao Cao shifted his focus to the independent kingdoms of the south, which he sought to bring back under imperial rule. By the spring of 208, he began construction of a new naval fleet that would allow him to project military forces into the south.[74] By summer an estimated 100,000 Wei troops set sail south down the Han River in an offensive campaign that culminated at Red Cliffs. Cao Cao's first major opponent was Liu Biao, Governor of Jing province, who controlled a significant portion of territory along the great Chang Jiang River, and more significantly, maintained an enormous flotilla of warships and an experienced riverine navy.[75] Liu Biao died in August, succeeded by his son, Liu Qi, whose advisors petitioned him to surrender his forces to Cao Cao and his rapidly approaching army.[76] Having no feasible alternative, Liu Qi surrendered his navy and soon afterwards fled with a group of dissidents eastward. The full strength of Liu Biao's exceptional military was now under the control of Cao Cao and comprised the bulk of the invasion force's navy.[77]

Continuing along the axis southward, the invasion force defeated and absorbed opposition armies, growing in size to 150,000 men or more.[78] The final size of the Wei force is still largely disputed with

---

[74] Lorge, "Naval Forces and Naval Operations," 85.

[75] di Crespigny, "The Three Kingdoms and Western Jin."

[76] *Ibid.*

[77] Zhang Xiugui, 214.

[78] Lorge, "Naval Forces and Naval Operations," 85.

estimates up to 240,000 soldiers and sailors along with thousands of assault ships.[79] Inspired by Lui Bei,

a member of the Han imperial family and one of the most renowned and celebrated warlords in Chinese

history, Li Qi fled eastward with Lui Bei's army and a group of dissidents to establish a line of defense to

slow Cao Cao's advance.[80] [See Appendix 1, Figure 2A] Moving to Jiangling, a key southern port city

and supply depot along the Chang Jiang, Liu Bei set into a defensive position north of the city.

Recognizing the strategic importance of Jiangling, Cao Cao deployed his force there to attack Liu Bei and

take the city as a base of operations for his southern offensive.[81] At the Battle of Changban, Cao Cao

soundly defeated Lui Bei's force, compelling Liu Bei and Liu Qi to seek a defensive alliance with the

southern kingdoms of Wu and Shu. Having established his new headquarters at Jiangling, Cao Cao sent

envoys ordering surrender to court of the king of Wu, Sun Ch'uan.[82]

Now fully understanding Cao Cao's intent, the kingdoms of Shu and Wu began negotiations to

establish a strategic alliance unified under a single military coalition to oppose the invasion into the south.

The details of this temporary alliance are illustrative of the fluid nature of politics and power sharing

during the Three Kingdoms era. In a calculated response to Cao Cao's order to surrender, Sun Ch'uan

ordered his forces, under the command of his cousin, the master strategist and general Zhou Yu, to

rendezvous with Liu Bei and Liu Qi at Red Cliffs in a joint effort to repel the Wei invasion in late

November 208. Sun Ch'uan's incentive for this course of action may have been to achieve a major

expansion of territory should the coalition repel Cao Cao's invasion.[83] He also was well aware that

surrender to Wei would end his kingdom's independent status. Regardless of motive, it was clear that

---

[79] Zhang Xiugui, 218.

[80] *The Cambridge History of China,* Denis Twichett and Michael Loewe, ed., (Cambridge: Cambridge University Press, 1986), 352.

[81] Rafe di Crespigny, "Generals of the South, " *The Foundation and Early History of the Three Kingdoms State of Wu,* Internet edition 2004, The Australian National University, 247. http://www.anu.edu.au/asianstudies/decrespigny/gos_ch4.pdf (accessed October 20, 2009),

[82] *Ibid,* "The Three Kingdoms and Western Jin: A History of China in the Third Century AD."

[83] *Ibid,* "Generals of the South."

only a unified alliance of southern forces could survive against the coming invasion. Estimates put the total strength of this allied contingent from 70,000 to 80,000.[84] Commanded by Zhou Yu and Liu Bei this combined force was aptly led and eager to stop the Wei incursion into their territory.

Although inferior in size to Cao Cao's forces, the coalition armies of Shu and Wu were more experienced at naval warfare, held the decisive high ground at Red Cliffs, and were fighting on their home territory for the fate of their kingdoms. These and several other important factors that favored the smaller allied force helped to negate some of Cao Cao's tactical advantages. The soft, marshy terrain along the middle Chang Jiang was unsuitable for effective employment of the Wei army's superb heavy cavalry, which performed poorly in the subtropical lands in the south.[85] Cao Cao's forces were exhausted from the long campaign and the march southward, and the overall Wei force, composed of imperial troops as well as defeated armies lacked cohesion. In contrast, most of the allied force, including the entire navy and the army under Zhou Yu was fresh and ready to fight. Additionally, a portion of the invasion army and most of the navy belonged to the late general Liu Biao, and these forces were distrustful and uncertain of their new leader, Cao Cao.[86] Furthermore, the Wei camp was struck by a plague that quickly spread to the main force, limiting the army's effectiveness and lowering its morale.[87] Finally, one of the most critical disadvantages for the Wei force was its general inexperience in naval warfare, since the army was predominantly composed of northerners and foot soldiers.[88] This lack of maritime expertise forced Cao Cao to exercise more caution that he had in previous operations.

Despite some of the advantages enjoyed by the allied defenders, Cao Cao's invasion army was still a very dangerous and highly capable threat. Cao Cao was an exceptional military strategist and a

---

[84] Zhang Xiugui, 218.

[85] Peers, 79.

[86] di Crespigny, "The Three Kingdoms and Western Jin."

[87] *Ibid*, "Generals of the South," 258.

[88] Zhang Xiugui, 215.

cunning leader whose lifetime of remarkable achievements is still celebrated in China today.[89] He was an extraordinary battlefield commander and could pull many disparate forces together into a single, coherent army.[90] In less than a decade, he was able to gain control of half of China in a brilliant series of military campaigns and through the creation of key political alliances. Cao Cao was also a shrewd diplomat and politician and was perhaps the only man in China with the genius, talent, and ambition to reunite the Han Dynasty. His invasion force going into the Red Cliffs campaign had the momentum of an already highly successful operation, spreading fear and uncertainty in the kingdoms of the south. Cao Cao had never lost a major engagement or campaign in his life when his flagship arrived at Jiangling. Most significantly, his army outnumbered its adversary by a ratio of at least three to one in both manpower and ships.

2. The Battle of Red Cliffs

Moving from his naval base at Jiangling sometime in December 208, Cao Cao and his invasion force headed towards Red Cliffs along two axes. His naval contingent sailed east on the Chang Jiang while a sizeable ground element marched along the most direct road from Jiangling to Red Cliffs.[91] Cao Cao sent his vanguard element ahead of the main body on foot to reconnoiter the allied force at Red Cliffs and possibly to make first contact with the enemy.[92] The allies were ready for this initial engagement, having prepared their armies for a coordinated defense on land. Considering Cao Cao's inexperience in naval warfare, allied strategists understood that he would likely attempt to unseat the allied position on the high ground at Red Cliffs without a naval engagement. Therefore, the first stage of the battle occurred on land, between the Wei vanguard and allied defenders, somewhere between Jiangling and Red Cliffs.[93]

---

[89] di Crespigny, "The Three Kingdoms and Western Jin."

[90] *Ibid*, "The Three Kingdoms and Western Jin."

[91] *Ibid*, "Generals of the South," 257.

[92] Zhang Xiugui, 218.

[93] *Ibid*, 218.

[See Appendix 1, Figure 2B] Entrenched in a prepared battle position and ready for Cao Cao's ground attack, this allied land contingent repelled and defeated the invasion force's advanced body, thus spoiling Cao Cao's strategy to destroy the allies by land.[94]

This small setback forced Cao Cao to deploy the armada and confront the allies in full force at Red Cliffs. As his invasion forces converged there, he emplaced his army on the northern bank of the Chang Jiang, striking camp and docking his naval forces opposite the allied navy of Liu Bei and Zhou Yu. The allied army remained entrenched in the high ground at Red Cliffs with their small but capable navy docked along the southern bank below.[95] Cao Cao's massive naval force anchored itself from stem to stern across its side of the river and chained together its ships to form a single, continuous wall.[96] Additionally, his force built wooden catwalks around these vessels to stabilize the entire navy from the rough current and to accommodate the northerners of his force who were unaccustomed to life on the water.[97] Both forces waited on their respective shores in a standoff that lasted several days, during which time Cao Cao's forces continued to amass greater strength from reinforcements while Zhou Yu and his allies deliberated on strategy to defeat this superior force.[98] Meanwhile, sickness continued to spread in the invasion army's camp, weakening the strength and morale of Cao Cao's force.[99]

This unusual standoff at the river's edge between Cao Cao and the allied forces marked a major transition in the course of the campaign. Although there was the initial ground component of the fighting west of Red Cliffs, the heart of the battle and the greatest loss of life occurred in the waters of the Chang

---

[94] di Crespigny, "Generals of the South," 257.

[95] *Ibid*, "The Three Kingdoms and Western Jin: A History of China in the Third Century AD."

[96] Lorge, "Water Forces and Naval Operations," 85.

[97] Ralph D. Sawyer, *Fire and Water: The Art of Incendiary and Aquatic Warfare in China*, (Boulder: Westview Press, 2004), 56

[98] di Crespigny, "Generals of the South," 259.

[99] The details of this "sickness" are uncertain. It may have been a plague or other infectious disease spread in the close quarters of the force's encampments. It is possible that the long march south and the climate of the south weakened the army, making the soldiers more susceptible to regional viruses to which they were not immune. See di Crespigny, "Generals of the South," 257.

Jiang. As he sat and waited with his massive naval force docked before him along the river's edge, Cao Cao rapidly lost the initiative, refusing to take offensive action against his adversary on the opposite side.[100] Although his reason for this delay remains unclear, there are three potential explanations for this uncharacteristic behavior. Cao Cao may have been convinced that the allied forces would lose heart at the terrible show of force of his armada and sue for peace. Waiting for a non-violent end to this confrontation would enable him to absorb the very capable forces of Shu and Wu into his army rather than destroy them. He may have been waiting for the conditions of weather and current to be more advantageous for attack. Some of his invasion force was still moving eastwards, and he may have sought to consolidate his entire force before beginning his assault. Regardless of the motive, Cao Cao's force sat docked and immobile only several hundred yards from an agile and well-trained adversary. This decision to delay the attack and lash his navy together into a single platform would lead to a disaster of legendary proportions.

The Battle of Red Cliffs was essentially a naval engagement, but the greatest killer of this battle was not the steel of the sword and arrow but fire. Incendiary warfare had become a major aspect of combat in the Late Han era. There were many cases when Chinese armies employed fire for military purposes long before the Battle of Red Cliffs.[101] By the time of the campaign the art of incendiary warfare in China had reached a new zenith and was becoming a decisive factor in warfare.[102] Techniques used by 208 CE included the use of fire ships, set ablaze and designed to ram into enemy ships, the firing of incendiary projectiles from bows, crossbows, and trebuchets, and the employment of a wide array of explosive devices.[103] Wooden ramparts and structures used for siege warfare and the wooden naval vessels of the era were particularly vulnerable to incendiary warfare.

---

[100] Sawyer, *Fire and Water*, 55
[101] *Ibid,* 10.
[102] *Ibid,* 52.
[103] *Ibid,* 63.

As the standoff between forces persisted with neither side willing to initiate an attack, the allies employed a new strategy. Taking advantage of weather conditions and favorable wind, the plan, devised by a strategist named Huang Gai, was to send an envoy to Cao Cao for surrender. Along with ten ships, this envoy would sail towards the Wei side pretending to seek a truce and negotiate terms of surrender. Filled with incendiaries and disguised, these ships left allied lines for Cao Cao's camp. By mid-river they were set ablaze and with strong winds to their sterns they rammed full force into their enemy's docked and fully immobile navy.[104] Within moments, the conflagration spread until it consumed the entire armada, sending Wei forces into panic and chaos. The effects of this deception were immediate. Thousands of Wei sailors perished by fire or drowning. Led by Zhou Yu, the second wave of the allied attack was comprised of infantry and cavalry, which conducted an amphibious assault on the Wei forces in disarray.[105] Those Wei soldiers and sailors that escaped the blaze were set upon by these allied ground forces, which had massed and deployed in full pursuit. The fleeing Wei soldiers were hacked down by the hundreds in the ensuing debacle.[106] Uncharacteristically, Cao Cao fled as well, doing little to organize or preserve those remaining in his force. When a rescue force arrived to save him from the blaze, he simply fled, leaving his army and navy at the mercy of the allied pursuers. A torrential downpour made the escape roads nearly inaccessible for the Wei force, thus adding to the totality of the allied rout.[107]

The strategic implications of this defeat were immediate. With much of his campaign force in ruins, Cao Cao and the survivors fled to their naval base at Jiangling. Allied pursuit halted short of Jiangling because of the large reserve force that the Wei army still had garrisoned there. The momentum and initiative from the campaign's many successes were lost forever at Red Cliffs. Cao Cao's invasion force was destroyed beyond repair, preventing any plans for counterattack. Leaving his garrison at

---

[104] di Crespigny, "Generals of the South," 257-258.

[105] *Ibid*, 258.

[106] Sawyer, *Fire and Water*, 58-59.

[107] *Ibid*, 59.

Jiangling, Cao Cao moved north to consolidate his gains in central China and to reorganize.[108] Thus the Wei campaign into the south of China was stopped and all hope for reunification of the southern kingdoms temporarily ended. The Red Cliffs Campaign was decisively concluded in a legendary confrontation that remains one of the greatest battles in all of Chinese military history.

D. Analysis

1. Orientation at the Strategic and Operational Levels of War

Analyzed from the perspective of the alliance of southern kingdoms, the Red Cliffs Campaign demonstrates the Chinese orientation towards the operational and strategic levels of war. Rather than attempting to defend against Cao Cao's invasion force with military power only, Liu Bei and his allies entered into a political coalition of southern kingdoms. In doing so they ensured the survival of their force and provided the means to defeat their numerically superior adversary. The leaders of the coalition focused on critical strategic objectives when designing the campaign, such as maintenance of the alliance and protection of its military forces. Despite their tactical inferiority, the allies understood the operational and strategic advantages they possessed when their adversary initiated his offensive. Cao Cao forced his invasion force to deploy deep into southern territory, allowing the allies marked advantages in the exploitation of terrain, operational depth, interior lines of communication, and simplicity of operational logistics. These helped mitigate their adversary's numerical superiority and tactical advantages. Although they ultimately defeated Cao Cao in a single tactical engagement, the allied strategic and operational focus allowed them to capitalize on some of their inherent advantages at the campaign level.

In contrast to the allied forces, Cao Cao failed to maintain strategic perspective in the Red Cliffs Campaign. His overall strategic objectives were to reunite the Han Dynasty by conquering the separate

---

[108] di Crespigny, "Generals of the South," 264.

36

kingdoms of the south and integrating them back into imperial rule. The campaign plan was to penetrate into the southern kingdoms, crush them individually through the threat or use of military force, and then force them into fealty to the empire. However, the design of his operation was overly ambitious and too focused on the military element of Wei's power. The commitment of such a large invasion force so deep into southern territory was a considerable strategic risk considering that the situation in central and north China was still somewhat volatile. This campaign in the south drew a substantial portion of his available military forces away from other important strategic requirements, such as protecting his imperial capital and safeguarding the frontier borders of the empire in the north and west.

In this campaign Cao Cao was overconfident in his invasion force's military advantages. This was evident in several of his key decisions that contributed to defeat, both tactically and operationally. By committing all of his forces in such a manner, Cao Cao allowed himself no tactical reserves, little space to maneuver, and no way to protect the campaign should he fail at Red Cliffs.[109] Rather than sitting immobilized with his army and navy encamped in a single spot, Cao Cao could have more effectively positioned his force, allowing the mutual support of units, greater dispersion and protection of the force, and a more ordered convergence of the army against the enemy. Since he focused on the tactical task of destroying the allied army, he failed to take into account important operational considerations and in doing so he made critical errors that jeopardized the campaign.

2. Strategic Maneuver Warfare

Recognizing Cao Cao's many tactical advantages, the allies performed exceptional strategic maneuver. Rather than facing their adversary on terrain of his choosing, the allies forced Cao Cao to come to them, making him deploy deeper into southern territory. This greatly stressed the logistical

---

[109] While he had an operational reserve ready at Jiangling, Cao Cao did not employ tactical reserves that he could have used during his enemy's assault at Red Cliffs.

capabilities of his campaign, physically exhausted his troops, and exposed them to unfamiliar terrain and climate. Since the allies could not survive in a land engagement against the full Wei army, which had far superior heavy cavalry, firepower, and infantry, they chose to defend from a position that would force Cao Cao to attack primarily with naval forces. Correctly assuming that he would first attempt to unseat them from their position by a ground attack with his vanguard forces, the allies created a defensive battle position on good terrain and executed a coordinated plan to defeat this initial assault. This successful operation prevented envelopment by land and enabled the allies to retain the decisive terrain at Red Cliffs. The excellent maneuver and positioning of allies in this early phase of the campaign negated Cao Cao's tactical advantages in ground warfare and made him rely on his navy, which was unfamiliar with the region, maintained only a marginal loyalty to their leader, and was unaccustomed to Wei military practices.

By forcing Cao Cao to commit his troops well into southern territory, the allies placed tremendous strain on the Wei force's ability to sustain itself in this long campaign. Far from its capital of Chang'an in north-central China, the invasion army was operating in territory over a thousand kilometers away from its base of power by land and several thousands of kilometers by river. [110] This heavily taxed the sustainment capabilities of the invasion force and placed significant limitations on their ability to stay afield for such a long duration. Cao Cao's impatience prevented him from taking important precautionary measures, such as allowing his force to acclimate to southern weather conditions and to familiarize with the operational environment. Added to the exhaustion of his force from the long movement, these errors contributed to the poor health of his army when it finally arrived at Red Cliffs. In short, the allied strategic maneuver forced Cao Cao to overextend his force operationally and logistically, which added greater complexity to Cao Cao's campaign and contributed to the overall failure of the invasion.

---

[110] Fairbank, *The Cambridge History of China: Volume 1, The Ch'in and Han Empires, 221 B.C.- A.D. 220*, 603. "Several thousand kilometers" is a rough estimate taken from the contemporary map of China on Google Maps, see http://maps.google.com/maps?source=ig&hl=en&rlz=1G1GGLQ_ENUS262&q=chibi%20china&um=1&ie=UTF-8&sa=N&tab=wl (accessed 28 January 2010).

In contrast, the allies operated in their home terrain and could sustain the coalition army with simple logistics and short lines of communication. Despite significant disadvantages, allied soldiers were fresh, properly motivated, and loyal to their leadership. They were familiar with the terrain and climate of the region and were experienced in the waters of the Chang Jiang and Han Rivers. Through strategic maneuver, the allies controlled the tempo and the direction of the campaign. Rather than facing the Wei invasion at the border of Wu, they chose to defend in depth, forcing Cao Cao to deploy in strength and exceed his force projection capabilities. Maneuvering in this manner, the allies were also able to select the decisive terrain of the region, Red Cliffs, and defend it with a much smaller force than the invading army.

3. Shaping Operations

In this campaign Cao Cao demonstrated an uncharacteristic lack of strategic patience, an important aspect of shaping operations. Key conditions were not set for the successful execution of this major military operation when he began the campaign. Although he had amassed a tremendous invasion force, he did not take the time to ensure that it was adequately prepared for combat operations in the south. As an experienced military commander with several successful campaigns in his career, Cao Cao must have understood the critical importance of command and control and training in warfare, especially when the major units comprising his force had never operated together. His invasion force lacked several key elements of military preparedness. Although he conducted some naval training prior to setting sail, he failed to properly integrate into his command the addition of Liu Biao's armada, which he acquired early in the campaign. The lack of sufficient naval training and the disunity of his subordinate units caused Cao Cao to take unwise precautions, such as lashing his navy together at Red Cliffs.

Apart from sending envoys demanding the surrender of the southern kingdoms, Cao Cao did little else to shape the conditions of the campaign in his favor. Had he focused more on non-military solutions for achieving his strategic objectives, he could have capitalized on the disunity and in-fighting of the southern kingdoms, which were constantly in conflict. By pitting the animosities of these kingdoms against each other, he could have achieved his subjugation of the south through alliance building and political intrigue rather than force alone. Cao Cao was a master statesman who excelled at political manipulation, yet uncharacteristically, in the Red Cliffs campaign he failed to exploit the potential for non-military means to achieve his goals in the south. Rather than sowing disunity in his adversaries by exploiting their inherent distrust of each other, Cao Cao's decision to take the southern kingdoms by force galvanized them against him.

The allied plan to defeat the Wei invasion force phased the operation in successive stages that each required the establishment of specific conditions. The first phase of the allied campaign was to deploy in depth and force Cao Cao to penetrate deep into southern territory and away from his regional base at Jiangling. Once Cao Cao moved in force from Jiangling, the allies could then repel his land assault through a well-prepared and coordinated defensive operation. This action would force Cao Cao to assault by river and unseat the allies from Red Cliffs through naval combat, for which they were better armed but less experienced. By shaping the conditions of the campaign in their favor, the allies were able to nullify many of the Wei army's advantages and better prepare their coalition army for defensive operations.

4. Deception and Unorthodox Warfare

The single most decisive factor in the allies' tactical victory at the Battle of Red Cliffs was the use of deception. Truly understanding the logic and motivations of the enemy commander, the allies took advantage of his overconfidence, his desire to take the allied armies intact and absorb them into his force, and his foolish decision to make his navy immobile. An element of Cao Cao's strategy in deploying most of his invasion force at Red Cliffs was likely to conduct a show of force that would dishearten the allied defenders and influence them to surrender. Several of his previous opponents in this and other campaigns had surrendered to him rather than face his army on the field. Liu Qi gave up his entire navy without a fight just months prior. It was likely that Cao Cao believed the allies would do the same, especially when confronted with the full might of the force before them. Knowing this, the allies exploited their enemy's arrogance through the execution of a masterful deception.[111]

The deception accomplished all that the allies had intended. It started a conflagration that destroyed the enemy's entire docked navy and its army encampments ashore. The smoke and fire of the spreading blaze killed or caused the drowning of thousands of Wei soldiers and sailors. Perhaps most significantly, the deception and the destruction it caused triggered a psychological panic in the invasion force that could not be diminished or contained. The exploitation attack that followed the deception capitalized on the havoc wreaked by the massive firestorm, allowing the allies to utterly destroy the fleeing survivors of the Wei force. The immediate effects of the deception were decisive and total. It enabled the allies to annihilate Cao Cao's army and navy and prevented any further continuation of the campaign. It forced Cao Cao and his remnants to flee back to Wei in defeat and prevented any future enemy incursions into the southern kingdoms for several decades. The allies needed a decisive victory over Cao Cao, and the use of deception provided them the means to achieve one.

E. Conclusion

The Red Cliffs Campaign provides an excellent case study of warfare in the Late Han era. This extraordinary event demonstrated the propensities of the Chinese art of war and remains today one of the truly great military operations of ancient Chinese history. The allied campaign plan remarkably captured the essence of the philosophies of Sunzi and several of the other great classic strategists. It emphasized the Daoist concept of *wu wei* in its strategy to defeat the invasion without overt confrontation and in the way the allies used elements that were inherent in the situation and the operational environment to their

---

[111] Cao Cao's overconfidence is evidenced in his failure to take any defensive precautions when accepting to his side Huang Gai's surrender and ten warships.

advantage. Fully understanding that they could not defeat Cao Cao in open battle on land, the allies allowed him to aggressively press his advantages and overextend his campaign. They artfully manipulated Cao Cao's operational oversights against him and used strategic maneuver to control the tempo and initiative of the campaign. The allies maneuvered and reshaped the battlefield to their advantage while Cao Cao allowed the loss of his campaign's momentum at Red Cliff to stifle his initiative.

The Red Cliffs Campaign showcases the Chinese emphasis on shaping operations and strategic maneuver and provides one of the greatest examples in world history of the effective use of deception in combat. What is additionally remarkable about this operation is that Cao Cao, a brilliant military commander and master politician, allowed himself to make so many uncharacteristic errors in his campaign plan. His earlier conquests in northern and central China reveal a general who was a master of operational art, an exceptional strategist, and a student of the classic military scholars. Yet at Red Cliffs this experienced commander allowed a greatly inferior military force to soundly destroy his military and ruin his campaign. Cao Cao's actions in this campaign were inconsistent with the Chinese way of war. Clearly he had diverged from the classic military principles and strategies that he had mastered earlier in his career. The Red Cliffs campaign provides a lesson in strategic patience and demonstrates what can happen when a military organization fails to consider the operational and strategic implications of its actions. It also reveals how ambition, overconfidence, and failure to understand one's adversary can contribute greatly to military disaster.

IV. Medieval Chinese Warfare: The Pamirs Expedition and the Battle of Talas (747-751 CE)

A. Introduction

The Pamirs Expedition and the Battle of Talas are a unique and remarkable military campaign in the history of medieval China. They were the results of the clash between two great rising empires of Asia, the newly formed Abbasid Caliphate of Arabia and the Tang Dynasty. This first operational campaign and only major battle in history between Arab and Chinese armies would establish the dominance of one culture in central Asia until the present day.[112] At the time, both of these civilizations were expanding in power, influence, and economic interests well beyond their traditional borders. The Abbasids were spreading Islamic culture and military power eastwards from Arabia while the Tang were looking to the west, expanding trade and territorial possessions into central and south Asia. The line of communication between these two great empires was the fabled "Silk Road," along which goods, information, and armies flowed between the worlds of East and West Asia.[113]

It was near this route in Central Asia, along the Talas River and within the borders of present day Kyrgyzstan that the armies of the Abbasid Caliphate and the Tang Dynasty met in a decisive battle that shaped the fate of the region. The Battle of Talas,[114] which ended China's four-year military campaign in Transoxania,[115] [See Appendix 3, Figure 4] was one of the great international military engagements of the era. The Chinese campaign across the Pamir Mountains and the historic clash at Talas pitted the expeditionary capabilities and military strategies of two formidable adversaries against one another. The

---

[112] Barry Hoberman, "The Battle of Talas," *Saudi Aramco World*, (September / October 1982), 26.

[113] Paul Lunde, "Muslims in China: The History," *Saudi Aramco World*, (July-August 1985), 2.

[114] Also called "The Battle of Talas River."

[115] Transoxania is the traditional name for the region of Central Asia between the Oxus (Amu Darya) and Jaxartes (Syr Darya) Rivers, bounded to the northwest by the Aral Sea.

results of the campaign determined which of the two civilizations would dominate this critical region of Central Asia, which lay directly between them.[116] The Battle of Talas was the last major clash of an extraordinary Chinese expeditionary campaign in Transoxania that began in 747. This four-year campaign and its final battle near the Talas River serve as an excellent example of Chinese military strategy, techniques, and tactics of the era. They showcase the modes and methods of warfare of medieval China as well as the continuities of its military traditions from antiquity.

B. Historical Setting

As with so many dynastic transitions in Chinese history, the end of the Sui Dynasty and beginning of the Tang in the seventh century was marked by several decades of violent internal conflict. The process by which the Tang came to replace the Sui was predominately a military one; the Tang were the most successful power on the battlefields for imperial succession.[117] After the first Tang emperor, Li Yuan, established succession of his house to the imperial throne in 618, the Tang began an impressive century-long campaign of unification and expansion.[118] However, it was Li Yuan's successor, the great Taizong, the second ruler of the Tang from 626 to 649, whose extraordinary achievements during this era are the most celebrated of the Tang Dynasty. Born in the year 600, Taizong was a nobleman who was trained in classic and historical learning and was an especially gifted military genius.[119] By the time he seized the throne in 626, he had established himself through military campaigning and political diplomacy as one of the greatest men of his age. After centuries of "dark ages"[120] in China, where disunity, civil

---

[116] Wassily Barthold, *Turkestan Down to the Mongol Invasion*, (London: Luzac and Company, 1968), 196.

[117] Graff, *Medieval Chinese Warfare*, 160.

[118] Later named Emperor Gaozu.

[119] Denis Twichett, ed., *The Cambridge History of China: Volume 3, Sui and T'ang China, 589-906,* Part I, (Cambridge: Cambridge University Press, 1979), 188.

[120] Daniel A. Foss, "Third and Sixth Century Crisis East and West," *World History Archive,* http://www.hartford-hwp.com/archives/55/046.html (accessed 9 December 09). The Chinese Dark Ages should not be confused with the Dark Ages of Europe, although both were somewhat contemporary. The Chinese Dark Ages

war, and weak imperial powers divided the civilization, Taizong united the disparate kingdoms of north and south China and created imperial institutions that would live on centuries after his death.[121] The mature and complex institutional practices adopted in the 7th and 8th centuries are described as "the age of bureaucracy" in China during which the imperial government exercised much greater control of state resources and the population.[122] The size of the government greatly expanded, creating new systems and oversight methods that enabled fuller use of the land and greater food production, expanded industry and trade, and more effective conscription and military capabilities.

Under Taizong, Tang armies embarked on an era of military expansion of China proper and well beyond, subduing the Korean peninsula, invading south into Vietnam, and spreading west into Central Asia.[123] In 626 he defeated a massive army of Turkic nomadic tribes that were massing along the Great Wall to invade into China from Central Asia, thus beginning a dramatic new series of westward imperial expansions well beyond the traditional borders of China.[124] During Taizong's reign, Chinese trade through the oasis cities of the Silk Road marked a new era of communication and interaction between the Chinese civilization and those in Central and Western Asia.[125] By the time of Taizong, the Tang had established relative peace within the kingdom but violent conflict continued along the borders and frontiers. The most significant of these enduring frontier conflicts were with the armies of the Eastern Turks.[126] The defeat of the Turks under the rule of Taizong enabled the Chinese to penetrate further north and west beyond the empire's borders.

---

occurred between 220 and 589 CE and began roughly from the collapse of the Han and ended with the advent of the Sui Dynasties.

[121] Lunde, "Muslims in China," 1.

[122] Michael Loewe, *Imperial China: The Historical Background to the Modern Age,* New York: Frederick A. Praegere Publishers, 1966), 61.

[123] John K. Fairbank, *China: A New History,* (Cambridge: Belknap Press, 1992), 78.

[124] Lunde, "Muslims in China: The History," 1.

[125] Fairbank, *China: A New History*, 78.

[126] Graff, *Medieval Chinese Warfare*, 185.

By the time of the Pamirs Expedition and the Battle of Talas, the westward extent of China's imperial power had reached well into Kabul and as far southwest as Kashmir, bringing the Tang into contact with the Muslim peoples of Turkestan and into conflict with their sovereigns in Arabia and Persia.[127] The Empire had achieved its greatest height in economic prosperity, military capabilities, and international influence under its fourth emperor Xuanzong (reigning from 713 to 755).[128] Imperial universities enrolled students from across the empire and beyond, and international envoys took note of Tang's imperial splendor and brought home with them Tang institutional innovations and ideas. The Japanese, for example, were so taken by the Tang state practices that the Japanese imperial court soon replicated Tang culture and government.[129] Eventually, however, the grandeur of the Tang Dynasty with its long international reach and expansive borders contributed significantly to its downfall. By the time of the Pamirs Expedition, as China was reaching new heights of imperial prosperity and greatness, signs of weakness were beginning to surface in many areas. The military was ruinously overextended with expensive campaigns in Central Asia and elsewhere draining critical manpower and imperial coffers, while leaving the heart of the empire and its capital dangerously unsecure.[130] Infighting and political intrigue within the imperial court led to a massive revolt, known as the An Shi Rebellion,[131] which nearly toppled the Tang Dynasty and signaled its impending decline.[132]

---

[127] Barry Hoberman, "The Battle of Talas," 26.

[128] Fairbank, *China: A New History*, 82.

[129] Ray Huang, *China a Macro History*, (New York: Eastgate, 1997), 101.

[130] Fairbank, *China: A New History*, 82.

[131] Also called the An Lushan Rebellion.

[132] Peers, *Imperial Chinese Armies: 200 BC - AD 1260*, 115.

C. The Campaign

1. The Pamirs Expedition (748-751 CE)

The great Tang Emperor, Taizong, and the Prophet Mohammed were contemporaries.[133] Four years before Taizong took the imperial throne of China in 626, Mohammed and his companions embarked on their great exodus, the *al-hegira,* from the holy city Mecca to Medina. Both the Tang Empire and the first Islamic Caliphate under the Prophet rose to greatness and power at about the same time, expanding their cultures and empires on opposite sides of Asia. Over the next hundred years, both civilizations increasingly came into contact and competition in Central Asia, setting the conditions for an eventual military clash. Control of the Silk Road into Central Asia was an important economic incentive for both empires. It bolstered international trade, increased technology sharing, and helped to spread influence and control beyond borders. Both the Chinese and Arab powers had growing diplomatic ties and political influence over Transoxania and the city-state principalities along the route. Since the defeat of the Western Turks by the Tang in the early eighth century, no new state had taken formal rule over the greater Turkestan, signaling an opportunity for both the Chinese and the Arabs to exert power in that region.[134]

In the first decade of the eighth century, the armies of the great Arab Muslim general, Qutaiba ibn Muslim crossed the Oxus River in modern day Turkmenistan, to take control of the Silk Road and to prepare for an invasion of China that never materialized.[135] At the same time, the Tibetan Kingdom, a neighbor and adversary of the Tang, was expanding through military force into China's sphere of influence in the southwest. As the Arab Caliphate pushed eastward into Persian and Turkic lands on China's western periphery and the Tibetan expansion threatened key Silk Road city-states southwest of

---

[133] Lunde, "Muslims in China: The History," 1.

[134] Barthold, *Turkestan Down to the Mongol Invasion,* 195.

[135] Lunde, 3.

the Tarim Basin, the Tang eventually were forced to respond with military power.[136] In 741, the situation

for the Chinese worsened as Tibetans crossed into the Oxus Valley and joined forces with the Arabs,

creating further impetus to raise a Chinese army for employment in that region.[137] That year, the Emperor

Xuanzong placed General Gao Xianzhi in command of a modest expeditionary force that would deploy to

recover Tang control of this area of contention beyond the Pamirs Mountains. The Pamirs, a region of

isolated high mountains predominately in modern day Tajikistan, lie at the crossroads of Central Asia,

linking China in the east to Kyrgyzstan, Pakistan, and Afghanistan.[138] With peaks ranging between

altitudes of 16,000 to 24,400 feet, this remarkable alpine range, called "the roof of the sun," lies at the

junction between the Hindu Kush and the Himalayas."[139]

The Pamirs Expedition, commanded by Gao Xianzhi, began in the spring of 748 and consisted of

a force of 10,000 Chinese cavalry and infantry from Anxi in the frontier region of the Tarim Basin in

northwest China. [See Appendix 3, Figure 5] Called the "Pivot of Asia" this expansive 350,000 square

mile basin of the Tarim River system lies predominately within modern day China's Xinjiang

autonomous region, but it also expands somewhat into several modern Central Asian states.[140] The

terrain feature that dominates more than half of the Tarim Basin is the Taklamakan Desert, China's

largest desert and the world's largest shifting sand desert.[141] General Gao was the deputy commander of

---

[136] Hoberman, "The Battle of Talas," 2.

[137] Aurel Stein, "A Chinese Expedition across the Pamirs and Hindukush, A. D. 747," *The Geographical Journal*, Vol. 59, No. 2 (Feb 1922), 115. Considered the "godfather" of archaeology in Chinese Turkestan, Sir Aurel Stein was a Hungarian archeologist whose explorations and studies of the Tarim Basin and the greater Silk Road regions continue to influence scholars today.

[138] Centre for Development and Environment, Swiss Agency for Development and Cooperation, *The Tajik Pamirs: Challenges of Sustainable Development in an Isolated Mountain Region*, (Berne: Geographica Bernensia, 2002), 6.

[139] Pamirs.org, "Pamirs," http://www.pamirs.org/ (accessed 2 February 2010).

[140] Mariner Padwa, "Archaeological GIS and Oasis Geography of the Tarim Basin," *The Silk Road Foundation Newsletter*, http://www.silk-road.com/newsletter/vol2num2/oasis.html, (accessed 2 February 2010).

[141] New Word Encyclopedia, "Takla Makan Desert," http://www.newworldencyclopedia.org/entry/Takla_Makan_Desert (accessed 2 February 2010).

the "Four Garrisons," the Tang army's frontier forces in the Basin.[142] Like many of his contemporary frontier commanders, Gao was not Han Chinese. His ancestral home was in the kingdom of Koguryo in northern Korea, and his father, Gao Shenji, had also served as a general under the Tang.[143] Rising through the ranks to general while still in his twenties, Gao Xianzhi had earned his reputation as an intelligent, experienced, and highly competent officer and commander. The Pamirs Expedition was an incredible four-year overland deployment of his force from the Tarim Basin, over the Pamirs Mountains, and into Transoxania, where Gao would wage a military campaign to reclaim control of this critical Silk Road region for the Tang Empire.[144]

The primary impetus for this military expedition was to deal once again with China's most formidable neighbor, the Kingdom of Tibet, which by 714 had expanded into regions under Tang suzerainty. In 722 the Tibetans invaded into Gilgit[145] and Baltistan, in modern-day northeast Pakistan, threatening the China's hold on these strategic crossroads of the Silk Road linking Kashgar to Kashmir and the Indus Valley.[146] Invaded by the Tibetans, the King of Gilgit appealed to the Tang, which sent a military expedition that liberated Gilgit and placed Baltistan back into Chinese control. Over the next two decades, hostilities between Tibet and Gilgit continued to flare until 741, when Tibetan offensives in the region required a new punitive response by the Tang. Further threatening Chinese control of the region was the Tibetan alliance with Arab forces, which had crossed the Oxus and Jaxartes Rivers and was increasingly taking control of Transoxania.[147] Thus, in 747, Gao Xianzhi took command of a new

---

[142] Stein, 116.

[143] Jonathan K. Skaff, "Barbarians at the Gates? The Tang Frontier Military and the An Lushan Rebellion," *Warfare in China to 1600,* Peter Lorge, ed., (Burlington: Ashgate, 2005), 399.

[144] Barthold, 195.

[145] Gilgit, also called "Little Balur" or "Lesser Bolu" was a tributary of China that became a client kingdom of the Tibetan Empire in 722. The subjugation of this city was the final state in the Tang pacification of the region. See Graff, *Medieval Chinese Warfare,* 213.

[146] *The Cambridge History of China Vol. 3,* Denis Twichett ed., 430-431.

[147] Oxus and Jaxartes are traditional names for the modern day Amu Darya and Syr Darya Rivers.

expeditionary force whose objectives were to establish Chinese control of the Gilgit region, build a base of operations there, and continue operations north into Transoxania.[148] [See Appendix 3, Figure 6A]

Gao's expedition began in the frontier garrison and headquarters at Anxi.[149] [See Appendix 3, Figures 6B to 6D] From there, Gao and his 10,000-man force moved west through the Taklamakan desert to the oasis city of Kashgar in a march that took thirty-five days. In order to expedite the movement of the army and facilitate logistics, Gao split the force into several columns, each taking separate routes across the Pamirs. Another twenty-day journey took the army southwest into the Pamir Mountain range to the Tang military outpost at Tashkurgan, where the force prepared for the crossing of the Pamirs into the border of modern-day Afghanistan.[150] Forty days later, Gao's column arrived at the Oxus River, in the Kingdom of Shinan. Stein described the impressive scope of this journey, which considering the technology of the day was truly an extraordinary feat. He wrote:

> The marching distance here indicated agrees well with the time which large caravans of men and transport animals would at present need to cover the same ground. But how the Chinese general managed to feed so large a force after once it had entered the tortuous gorges and barren high valleys beyond the outlying oases of the present Kashgar and Yangihissar districts is a problem which might look formidable, indeed, to any modern commander...The crossing of the Pamirs by a force which in its total strength amounted to ten thousand men is so remarkable a military achievement that the measures which alone probably made it possible deserve some closer examination, however succinct the Chinese record is upon which we have to base it.[151]

At Shinan, Gao split his force again, this time into three columns and deployed in tactical formation southwest to maneuver against the Tibetans along the Oxus River valley. With his columns converging at Sarhad, Gao crossed the Oxus and assaulted a Tibetan force in defensive positions. Maneuvering to his enemy's flank, Gao achieved a tactical envelopment, in which he gained the key high ground on the battlefield and was able to penetrate the Tibetan defenses and destroy the enemy line in

---

[148] *The Cambridge History of China Vol. 3,* 433.

[149] Stein, 117.

[150] *Ibid,* 117.

[151] *Ibid,* 118.

detail. [152] Gao's force continued towards the Tibetan fortress of Lien-yun near Sarhad. There he formed

ranks and assaulted uphill against a large Tibetan force defending from a mountain fortress. The five-

hour battle was a great victory for the Tang forces, which killed 5,000 men and captured another 1,000. [153]

Having secured the Oxus River Valley and destroyed the Tibetan units stationed there, Gao left a

detachment at Lian-yun and proceeded with his main force south, moving downwards in elevation into

the Yasin Valley. There he pacified the remaining Tibetans in the area and continued south to Gilgit, at

the border between modern-day Pakistan and Kashmir, where he established Tang control, installed a

permanent garrison, and retired his force for the winter. [154]

Victorious, and with his army firmly in control of the region, General Gao returned to the

imperial capital with captives from the expedition. [155] From a strategic perspective, this campaign's

victory accomplished two critical tasks. It put an end to Tibetan aggression in the region and claimed the

petty kingdoms of the southern Pamirs for the Tang. It cut the Tibetans' communications with their Arab

allies, lessening the threat of coordinated attacks on Tang interests in Transoxania. [156] The scale and

significance of Gao Xianzhi's incredible accomplishment in crossing the Pamirs and defeating the

Tibetan forces is best described by Stein, who retraced parts of Gao's journey during visits to the region

from 1906 to 1916. According to Stein's observation,

> If judged by the physical difficulties encountered and vanquished, the achievement of the able
> Korean General deserves fully to rank by the side of the great alpine feats of commanders famous
> in European history. He, for the first, and perhaps the last, time led an organized army right
> across the Pamirs and successfully pierced the great mountain rampart that defends Yasin-Gilgit
> and with it the Indus valley against invasion from the north. Respect for the energy and skill of
> the leader must increase with the recognition of traditional weakness which the Annals'
> ungarnished account reveals in his troops. [157]

---

[152] *Ibid*, 121.

[153] *Ibid*, 120.

[154] *Ibid*, 129.

[155] *Ibid*, 129-130.

[156] Graff, *Medieval Chinese Warfare,* 213.

[157] Stein, 112 and 130.

2. The Battle of Talas (751 CE)

The extraordinary journey of Gao's expeditionary force so far beyond the furthest reaches of the Tang Empire, across the Pamirs into the icy foothills of the Hindu Kush, and its three years of successful military campaigning in Transoxania were truly remarkable feats.[158] But the army would soon be tested again, and this time by an enormous Arab coalition deployed for battle. By 751, Gao had been appointed the military governor of Anxi and was highly successful in his control of the Tarim Basin and the new Tang possessions in the Pamirs, Kashmir, and the south Oxus valley. His influence had spread as far west as Kabul and deep into the principalities of central and north Transoxania, which included Ferghana, Samarkand, Tashkent, and some other city-states north of the Jaxartes.[159] Described by Graff as "ill-starred," the year 751 had been remarkably bad for the Tang Empire with military disasters against Tibetans in Sichuan in the southwest and against Khitan forces in the north.[160] The Tang control of its frontier provinces would be further threatened in the late summer of the same year at the Talas River. [See Appendix 3, Figure 7]

The conflict that would end decisively at the Battle of Talas began as local quarrel between the petty kingdoms of Ferghana and Tashkent, two important Silk Road city-states along the Jaxartes River valley in modern-day Uzbekistan. General Gao chose to intervene with military force on behalf of Ferghana and besieged the city of Tashkent.[161] The Chinese forces captured the king of Tashkent, and Gao had him executed "for the non-fulfillment of his duties as vassal."[162] Enraged, the son of the overthrown king of Tashkent sought aid from the Abbasid governor of Khorashan, abu Muslim, who saw

---

[158] Stein,130.

[159] Also called "Chach" or "Shash."

[160] Graff, *Medieval Chinese Warfare,* 214-215.

[161] *Ibid,* 215.

[162] Bartold, 195.

an opportunity to diminish China's influence in Central Asia.[163] A large Muslim force, under the

command of Ziyad ibn Salih, the former Umayyad governor of the holy city of Kufa and the new regent

of Samarkand, assembled at the town of Merv[164] in present-day Turkmenistan and deployed north,

crossing the Jaxartes River to confront the Chinese.[165] Reinforced with additional troops from

Turkharistan, Ziyad's coalition army was estimated at 100,000 men.[166] By July of 751, Gao's force

assembled near the town of Talas.[167] His army was supplemented with troops from Ferghana and a large

contingent of Qarluk Turks.[168] The total size of the Gao's coalition army at Talas numbered

approximately 10,000 Chinese and 20,000 Qarluk Turks.[169]

Although this was the first and only major military engagement between Arab and Chinese

armies, the tactical details of the actual battle are somewhat sparse. Both armies assembled near the Talas

River and formed for battle. The Chinese faced a vastly superior force. The fighting that ensued may

have lasted for up to five days.[170] During the battle, the Qarluk Turks, who were allied with the Chinese

and composed two-thirds of Gao's coalition, defected to the Arab side, contributing to the total defeat of

the Chinese.[171] One account suggests that this was a premeditated mutiny arranged by Ziyad and the

Qarluk Turks before the fighting.[172] Regardless, the battle resulted in a total rout of the Chinese force, in

---

[163] Hoberman, 3.

[164] Merv is located near the present day city of Mary, Turkmenistan.

[165] Hoberman, 3.

[166] Lunde, 3.

[167] Talas is the present day city of Taraz in Kazakhstan.

[168] Graff, *Medieval Chinese Warfare,* 215.

[169] Stein,118.

[170] Lunde, 3.

[171] Graff, *Medieval Chinese Warfare*, 215.

[172] Hoberman, 3.

which Gao and a small remnant of Chinese barely escaped.[173] The Battle of Talas was conclusively an Arab tactical and strategic victory that had enormous significance to the future of the region.

In the words of the great Russian historian, Wassily Bartold, "The Battle of Talas is undoubtedly of great importance in the history of Turkestan as it determined the question of which of the two civilizations, the Chinese or the Muslim, should predominate the land."[174] In the preceding years, the Chinese were unable to raise a new army to oppose the Arabs in Transoxania because the An Shi Rebellion, which began four years after the Battle of Talas, posed a greater strategic threat to the Tang Empire, necessitating the redeployment of all available military forces back into China's interior.[175] Thus, after Talas, Arab influence and control west of the Pamirs was able to spread without opposition from China, firmly establishing the dominance of Muslim culture in the region to the present day.

D. Analysis

The Pamirs Expedition and the Battle of Talas shed interesting light on the commander of both campaigns, General Gao Xianzhi. What is so fascinating about these operations is that they shared the same commander and army but had two vastly different outcomes. The Pamirs Expedition was a resounding operational and strategic success for both Gao and the Tang Empire. In a single campaign, a Chinese army was able to put the regional aspirations of a formidable adversary, the Kingdom of Tibet, in check. The Expedition succeeded in projecting strategic power across the Pamirs, opening a new sphere of influence for the Empire and providing many economic and strategic benefits, including control of the Silk Road into the Indus Valley and Afghanistan. It also propelled Gao to the position of regional governor, giving him greatly enhanced political and military power from the Tarim Basin to Transoxania

---

[173] Stein, 131.

[174] Bartold, 196.

[175] Twichett and Fairbank, *The Cambridge History of China, Volume 3, Sui and T'ang China, 589-906,* 443-444.

and the Hindu Kush. The Battle of Talas, occurring only three years after the Pamirs Expedition, was an operational and strategic disaster for both Gao and the Tang Empire. In a single campaign, Gao lost his army and China lost its foothold into Transoxania and Central Asia forever. These events beg an important question: How can a commander who accomplished so extraordinary a task, one that has never before or since been duplicated by a Chinese Army, be utterly defeated in a single battle only three years later?

The Pamirs Expedition and the Battle of Talas are in many ways a tale of two commanders: Gao Xianzhi the campaign commander and operational artist and Gao Xianzhi the regional warlord. The four years between 748 and 751 detail a senior Chinese military officer's descent into warlordism. Before the Pamirs Expedition, Gao was newly promoted to the position of expeditionary commander. He was eager for the opportunity to showcase his skill and talent. He was an operational commander working in support of his Empire's strategic objectives. In this role as commander of the Pamirs Expedition, Gao demonstrated exceptional audacity and a masterful understanding of the art and science of warfare at the campaign level. His movements were well-planned and orchestrated, demonstrating his unmatched expertise in strategic logistics. After his victory, he returned to the Tang capital with the spoils of his campaign, signifying his loyalty and subordination to his empire.

After the Pamirs, we see a different Gao Xianzhi. Victorious and greatly celebrated by his empire, he was given the promotion to military governor of Anxi, which for a non-Han was the highest position possible in the ranks of the Tang government. In this position he was granted relative autonomy over the Tarim Basin and lands west and south of the Pamirs. He was responsible for new frontier garrisons in Transoxania and for managing the vassal city-states of the Silk Road. Like so many of his predecessors with similar power, Gao Xianzhi devolved from military commander to regional warlord. Full of power and overconfidence, Gao began to exhibit behavior that was inconsistent with his previous record. His operational military actions were reckless and impatient. His warlordism was evidenced in his heavy-handed approach to governorship of his tributary kingdoms. Choosing to resolve the dispute between Ferghana and Tashkent with unilateral military force rather than through diplomacy, Gao caused multiple unforeseen consequences that would contribute to his downfall. His behavior as governor of Anxi suggests an inability to foresee or prepare for the possibility of intervention in the region by the Arabs. It is possible that he was simply blinded by his personal aims in the region, as was the case for so many warlords in Chinese history. In short, once he became a regional warlord, he stopped working in support of his empire's strategic objectives and began operating in support of his own. Evidenced by his behavior after his great victory in the Pamirs Expedition, it was clear that Gao's focus was on growing his own private kingdom and not on the strategic implications of his actions. This was precisely how a brilliant military commander went from unequaled achievement to total disaster in only four years.

1. Orientation at the Strategic and Operational Levels of War

During the Pamirs Expedition, Gao Xianzhi's behavior was consistent with the Chinese propensity of orientation at the strategic and operational levels of war, resulting in a great strategic victory for the Tang Empire. Although the tactical components of this operation were impressive given that the movement of a large military force over the Pamirs is no minor feat, the campaign's ultimate significance lay in its strategic importance to the Tang Empire. The projection of this military force beyond the mountains into Transoxania, Afghanistan, and Kashmir had enormous strategic implications. First, the movement was unprecedented, as no large Chinese army had ever accomplished or even attempted a crossing of the Pamirs before. It extended Chinese military power into new strategically important regions that helped to control commerce along the Silk Road into South and Central Asia. Additionally, it countered Tibetan strategic movements against the Tang and denied them critical resources in the Oxus River Valley and the Kingdom of Gilgit.

Gao was successful because he conducted this campaign with the purpose of achieving his empire's strategic goals, which were to check Tibetan activity in Gilgit, establish military control west of the Pamirs, and to create a new governorship of the region under the Tang. Gao focused on these strategic military objectives and designed his campaign to achieve them. His orientation at the strategic and operational levels of war enabled him to not only cross the Pamirs but to maneuver his forces in support of its subsequent operational objectives. In this campaign, Gao demonstrated a true mastery of the operational art, linking and integrating the tactical tasks of the mission together to achieve his operational objectives.[176] Throughout the operation, Gao's behavior revealed a commander who was focused on the accomplishment strategic endstates and who subordinated himself and his army to the political leadership of his empire.

In the Battle of Talas, Gao Xianzhi's behavior was inconsistent with the Chinese emphasis on the accomplishment of strategic and operational objectives, resulting in his catastrophic defeat and the loss of all the strategic gains he had previously achieved for the empire. Gao lost sight of the strategic level of war, which must be subordinate to the objectives of the political leadership of the state. Operating in his own interest and without supervision from his state government, he failed to adequately prepare his military forces for the possibility of intervention by a strong foreign power. Gao's three years of campaigning in Transoxania must have alerted him to the threat that the Caliphate posed to his control of the region. Arab military forces had been present in the region for nearly fifty years prior to the Battle of Talas. Additionally, Gao had not firmly established the loyalty of his new vassal city-states, who were clearly waiting to see which of the powers would become the region's hegemon.

Gao's defeat at the Battle of Talas was an outcome of his failure to focus on strategic considerations. This failure left him wholly unprepared, militarily and politically, for the Arab challenge to his region. His behavior prevented him from properly administering his new governorship as a protectorate of the Tang Empire. Gao's unilateral and heavy-handed approach to control of his

---

[176] U.S. Army doctrine defines the operational art as "the employment of military forces to attain strategic and/or operational objectives through the design, organization, integration, and conduct of strategies, campaigns, major operations, and battles. Operational art translates the joint force commander's strategy into operational design, and, ultimately, tactical action, by integrating the key activities at all levels of war." See *FM 1-02, Operational Terms and Graphics*, page 1-138.

tributaries, such as his execution of the King of Ferghana, must have led to the kind of distrust and dissention that motivated the betrayal of the Qarluk Turks during the battle. He was operating in support of his own personal objectives, and this directly led to his overconfidence, his poor political leadership, and his inability to adequately prepare against a real military threat to the region. Focusing on the strategic and operational levels of war enabled Gao Xianzhi to accomplish extraordinary tasks with his army. Disregarding strategic objectives in favor of personal ones contributed to the debacle at Talas and the utter destruction of that same army.

2. Strategic Maneuver Warfare

During the Pamirs Expedition, Gao's army demonstrated exceptional strategic maneuver. His campaign plan was to conquer Tibetan territories with only a moderate force through an expertly planned military campaign focused on maneuver. His strategy was not attritional or positional warfare as he had neither the forces nor the time to accomplish either. Instead, he planned a phased operation, focused on the achievement of operationally significant intermediate objectives that were integrated into a focused and synchronized campaign plan. This campaign plan revealed much about Gao's understanding of complex operational considerations in warfare, such as the proper execution of key logistical tasks associated with force projection over such a distance, the sequencing of lines of operation, control of the tempo of the campaign, and most significantly, the focus on campaign endstates. By coordinating these many critical tasks, Gao was able to accomplish extraordinary feats that were sequenced in a deliberate manner.

The maneuver of this army was organized into distinct, sequential phases. Each phase oriented on strategic endstates and built on the successful accomplishment of the previous phase. Gao's first march objective was to achieve the crossing of the Pamirs with his force intact. This required the movement of this force from its start point in Anxi, through the desert to the oasis city of Kashgar, across the initial mountain passes to the frontier outpost at Tashkurgan, and finally, the most difficult movement across the peak and into the Oxus River valley via multiple mountain passes. His next phase was to initiate combat operations against the Tibetans down the Oxus River valley to the mountain stronghold at Sarhad. In this phase, Gao maneuvered his force in tactical formations, enabling a coordinated convergence at Sarhad from three directions. The final phase involved the movement of the force southwards into Gilgit, the pacification of that kingdom, and the establishment of permanent frontier bases from which to launch future offensive operations into Transoxania. These effective operational maneuvers accomplished two important strategic tasks, the isolation of Gilgit and the severing of the line of communication between the Tibetans and the Arabs.

Unlike in the Pamirs Expedition, Gao failed to execute strategic maneuver before or during the Battle of Talas. In fact, he performed no maneuver except for consolidating his entire expeditionary force, without operational reserves, at a single battlefield. It is no surprise that he was soundly defeated by the much larger Arab army, as he had failed to provision for any operational depth in the arrangement of his forces, had no way to reinforce his army or exploit successes on the battlefield, and did not ensure the loyalty of his coalition army. Why he even attempted to fight at Talas against so large a force is uncertain. Either he had no choice but to fight the Arabs, which would suggest that he had poorly maneuvered his force such that they could not withdraw from the battlefield, or he was confident of victory, even when he was outnumbered at least three to one and most of his forces were non-Chinese. The latter suggests overconfidence in his generalship, misjudgment of the integrity of his coalition, and an underestimation of his adversary's strength and capabilities.

Gao's major defeat at Talas is due in part to his failure to perform strategic maneuver. While he may have attempted to tactically deploy his army on the battlefield at Talas, he failed to conduct adequate operational or strategic maneuver before the battle. His smaller force could have defeated this large Arab invasion, had he maneuvered in a manner that was strategically advantageous to his force, such as establishing a defense-in-depth on battle positions situated on key terrain. Gao's previous performance against the Tibetans in the Oxus River Valley demonstrated his understanding of strategic maneuver.

Why he failed to properly deploy his forces before the engagement at Talas might again be attributed to his unfortunate transformation from operational commander to regional warlord and the subsequent shift in his focus from strategic objectives and strategic maneuver to opportunism.

Another factor that may have strongly affected the different outcomes of the campaigns against the Tibetans and the Arabs was each of these adversaries possessed greatly different capabilities. The Arab army under Ziyad ibn Salih was 100,000 strong, all of which were assembled on a single battlefield. Ziyad's army was a campaigning army, designed for mobile warfare and on the offensive. The Tibetans that Gao faced were dispersed across several defensive positions and many hundreds of miles. They were much smaller in number and capability than the Arabs.

3. Shaping Operations

Shaping operations played a critical role in the Pamirs Expedition and were vital to the success of the campaign. An important factor in shaping the conditions for the expedition was the preparation and planning for operational logistics to sustain the force over such a long and complex movement. His traversing of the mountain passes in multiple columns suggests a very well-ordered logistical plan. Gao's force of 10,000 included 3,000 cavalry and several thousand baggage ponies. While these animals provided mobility and bore much of the weight in equipment and supplies, they also complicated logistics. At altitudes of over 16,000 feet, most of the mountain passes in the Pamirs crossing provided insufficient grazing opportunities for the army's many horses and pack animals.[177] For this and other reasons directly relating to operational logistics, Gao moved his force through multiple avenues of approach, speeding the movement of the force and maximizing available outpost supplies and local provisions until the army descended into the more fertile Oxus River valley.

---

[177] Stein, 117.

In addition to outstanding logistical planning, Gao further shaped the conditions of the campaign by phasing his operation in sequential stages. Establishing critical march objectives, each leg of the movement and each route had a purposeful endstate, creating the conditions that facilitated each subsequent phase. This enabled better command and control over his force, which was dispersed along many axes. By shaping the operational environment to best support his force, Gao and his army were able to descend across the Oxus, over the Dariot Glacier, and onto Tibetan positions in the Hindu Kush and the Indus River Valley. Throughout the expedition, Gao displayed the tactical patience, ingenuity, and expertise of a seasoned alpine campaign commander who understood the critical importance of operational planning and conditions setting.

Unlike in his deliberate and methodical crossing of the Pamirs and Hindu Kush, General Gao failed to shape any of the conditions of the campaign before the Battle of Talas. At the strategic level, his approach to governing his newly acquired vassals in Transoxania failed to solidify his foreign allies in the region. This led to his inability to raise any more than 20,000 non-Chinese soldiers to fight in his army and may have also contributed to the defection of the Qarluk Turks during the battle. Unlike his adversary's commander, Ziyad ibn Salih, Gao went into a major battle without fully consolidating his coalition. The Arab army, consisting of a mix of Muslim peoples including Arabs and Turks, were unified for battle. Gao also failed to ensure the commitment of his empire's resources before the battle. Perhaps not wishing to draw the attention of the central government to his warlord activities in the west, Gao went into battle with only the 10,000 Chinese troops he had on hand.

At the operational level Gao failed to set critical conditions for the success of his army. He established no operational reserve in the region. When he lost the battle, all of his forces west of the Pamirs were utterly destroyed, save a small remnant of survivors including Gao. An experienced campaign commander such as Gao should have known the importance of operational reserves, which can be committed into battle to exploit successes or to reinforced weaknesses. That he was lured into battle against a force three times the size of his suggests that he failed to establish any form of counterreconnaissance to provide early warning of enemy movement in his area of operations. His failure to perform critical shaping operations contributed significantly to the defeat of the Chinese force. At the Battle of Talas, Gao Xianzhi lost because he allowed himself to blunder into a major combat operation against a vastly superior enemy far from his base of operations, without adequate support and without setting the conditions for success at the tactical and operational levels of war.

4. Deception and Unorthodox Warfare

While the use of deception did not play a major role in the Pamirs Expedition, the element of surprise and the psychological effect of deploying so large a military force from China across the Pamirs against the unsuspecting Tibetan forces was clearly an important part of Gao's operational design. One can imagine the surprise and horror of the Tibetan defenders at Sarhad as they witnessed 10,000 Chinese infantry and cavalry converging on their position from three avenues of approach. Crossing the Pamirs with a Chinese army had never before been attempted until this expedition. Tibetans in Gilgit had no reason to prepare for any Chinese military reaction to their activities south of the Pamirs. Judging by Gao's rapid conquest of the Oxus valley, Gilgit, and Kashmir, it is clear that the Tibetans were taken fully by surprise in this Chinese invasion. Being so psychologically rattled and physically unprepared to defend, the Tibetans were quickly defeated in a single campaign season at little cost to the Chinese expeditionary force. Gao's brilliant planning and the sheer audacity of this operation contributed significantly to the success of the campaign.

At the Battle of Talas, deception seemed to play no role in Gao's battle plan. In fact, he himself was deceived by the Qarluk Turks and betrayed in the midst of the fighting. Rather than surprising his adversary with some clever deception, Gao was caught unprepared for the size and strength of the Arab army. One must question how a commander could employ the element of surprise so masterfully and to such great effect in one campaign and yet fail entirely to do so in the next major campaign. The fact that the effective use of deception in warfare requires significant planning, a deep understanding of one's adversary, and a great deal of preparation and rehearsal suggests that Gao was caught totally unprepared for all of the events leading to the Battle of Talas.

E. Conclusion

The Pamirs Expedition and the Battle of Talas provide excellent insight into the art and science of frontier warfare during the Tang Dynasty. This campaign reveals continuities in the martial traditions of ancient China to its medieval era as well as new innovations and evolutions in the Chinese way of war. It shows that warfare in China is not stagnant, but dynamic, adapting and evolving as technology and the operational environment changed. Yet despite the new modes and methods of war and the growing requirements of an expanding empire, the four propensities of the Chinese way of war continued to exist in medieval China and its armies continued to be influenced by the philosophies of Sunzi and the classic strategists of ancient China.

A remarkable aspect of the Pamirs Expedition and the Battle of Talas is that its commander, General Gao Xianzhi, both followed and diverged from the propensities of Chinese warfare in sequential campaigns, and this variable behavior had tremendous impact on the operation. When Gao acted as a true operational commander, subordinate to his empire and focused on its strategic objectives, he succeeded in accomplishing what no other general in China was able to achieve. Orienting at the strategic and operational levels of war, Gao was able to achieve the objectives of his empire. Employing extraordinary maneuver warfare and shaping the conditions of war in his favor, he soundly defeated the Tibetan forces in the Pamirs and Hindu Kush. However, when he acted as a regional warlord, working in his own interests and diverging from important military traditions of China, his army was destroyed in a single battle and the gains that he achieved for his empire were lost forever.

The next segment of this work looks at warfare in China's modern era with a history of the Chinese People's Volunteer Force in Korea during China's First and Second Phase Offensives of 1950 and provides an analysis of the Chinese way of war in modern history.

V. Modern Chinese Warfare: The Chinese Korean War Offensive of 1950 (October to December 1950)[178]

A. Introduction

Beginning in October 1950, China's intervention on the side of North Korea during the Korean War was a major turning point that strategically escalated the conflict, fundamentally changing the nature of the war from a United Nations sectioned "police action" to a major conventional war between the United Nations Command (UNC) led by the United States and North Korean forces supported heavily by the People's Republic of China. Badly mauled by US airpower and caught in an envelopment between the UN forces attacking from Inchon and pushing north from Pusan, the North Korean People's Army (NKPA) conducted a disorganized retreat north of the 38th Parallel in late September 1950, which signaled the beginning of the end of the war in the minds of several key American commanders.[179] Self-assured of rapid and decisive victory, General Douglas MacArthur, the Commander in Chief of UNC, disregarded the threat of Chinese intervention and ordered his forces to attack deep into North Korea. MacArthur's "heady optimism" and "home for Christmas" mentality was soon shattered by a massive Chinese surprise counteroffensive in November, consisting of the Chinese People's Volunteers (CPV), aptly commanded by Marshall Peng Dehuai.[180] In a matter of days, the Chinese intervention transformed the conflict, in MacArthur's words, into "an entirely new war."[181]

---

[178] The official name of this campaign was the "First and Second Phase Offensives." American histories of the Korean War often refer to it as the Chinese Offensive of 1950, the Chinese Intervention, the First Chinese Offensive, or the First Chinese Counteroffensive. This operation is best known for its most famous battle, the Battle of Chosin Reservoir (also called the Changjin Lake Campaign), fought between the Chinese People's Volunteers and UNC forces from 25 November to 24 December 1950.

[179] Alexander L. George, *The Chinese Communist Army in Action: The Korean War and its Aftermath*, (New York: Columbia University Press, 1967), 1.

[180] Richard W. Stewart, *Staff Operations: The X Corps in Korea, December 1950,* (Ft. Leavenworth: Combat Studies Institute, 1991), 2. The Chinese People's Volunteers is also referred to in historical texts as the People's Volunteer Army (PVA), Chinese People's Volunteer Force (CPVF), or the People's Volunteer Force

Caught wholly unprepared for a Chinese attack of this magnitude, US forces faced near destruction and were compelled to conduct the longest retreat in US military history.[182] Had it not been for the extraordinary tactical leadership and tenacious fighting spirit exhibited by Soldiers and Marines of the US X Corps and Eighth Army, the UN counteroffensive north of the 38th Parallel in 1950 might have ended in a total catastrophe. China's 1950 offensives in North Korea against the UNC from October to December 1950, also called the "First and Second Phase Offensives" by the Chinese high command,[183] provides an extraordinary glimpse into modern Chinese warfare. It sheds unique insights into the strategy, operational art, and tactics employed by the PLA in its first major engagement with a Western power. This campaign is illustrative of the Chinese way of war in the modern era, and it reveals continuities in the four propensities of Chinese warfare. Ultimately, these major Chinese offensives prevented the total collapse of the North Korean government and the destruction of its army. By clearing UN forces from North Korea, the campaign enabled a continuation of the war for another two and a half bloody years until the signing of the Korean Armistice Agreement in July 1953. This was the first war since the founding of the People's Republic of China on 1 October 1949, and it greatly accelerated PLA modernization.

B. Historical Setting

The CPV's First and Second Phase Offensives were a major turning point in the Korean War, which began on 25 June 1950 when the North Korean People's Army crossed the 38th parallel and invaded the Republic of Korea. By 27 June, the United Nations passed two U.S. sponsored resolutions to

---

(PVF). Some US military publications reference Chinese military forces in Korea as Chinese Communist Forces (CCF).

[181] Xiaobing Li, *A History of the Modern Chinese Army,* (Lexington: The University Press of Kentucky, 2007), 80.

[182] George, 2.

[183] Eric M. Hammel, *Chosin: Heroic Ordeal of the Korean War,* (New York: The Vanguard Press, 1981), 5.

denounce North Korea as an aggressor, render assistance to the Republic of Korea, and restore international peace on the peninsula.[184] The NKPA initiated their attack with a massive three-pronged armored thrust aimed at Seoul, nearly destroying three ROK divisions and sending the remaining ROK forces into a disorganized southward retreat.[185] By the following week, the smaller and more poorly armed ROK army was nearing collapse. After an operational pause following the capture of Seoul, NKPA forces continued the offensive southwards as the United States struggled to deploy the 24th Infantry Division and bring follow-on divisions to the peninsula in July. By the end of month, U.S. and ROK forces, now under the command of Lieutenant General Walton Walker's Eighth Army, had withdrawn to the Pusan Perimeter in the southwestern corner of the peninsula, fighting a fierce six-week series of defensive battles against a committed and numerically superior North Korean force.

In one of the greatest operational maneuvers of the twentieth century, MacArthur's audacious plan for an amphibious landing deep behind NKPA's rear, code-named Operation Chromite, turned the tide of the war. On 15 September 1950, the US X Corps successfully landed unopposed at Inchon, maneuvering directly to liberate Seoul and isolate the dispersed NKPA from the north. Simultaneously Walton's Eighth Army began its counteroffensive to break out of the Pusan Perimeter and attack the retreating NKPA. [See Appendix 4, Figure 8B] Caught between the anvil of X Corps in the north and the hammer of Eighth Army, the ensuing UN counteroffensive was an extraordinary success, destroying most of the remnants of the NKPA save 25,000 troops that were able to flee north of the 38th Parallel.[186] By 19 October UNC had crossed the 38th Parallel and captured the North Korean capital, Pyongyang. All that remained was a clean-up effort to destroy the remnants of the NKPA, and the war would be over.

By this time MacArthur and his staff in the General Headquarters Far East Command (GHQ FEC) had severely underestimated the intentions, capabilities, and military skill of the Chinese, whom

---

[184] Hastings, 60.

[185] Fehrenbach, 35.

[186] *Ibid*, 180.

many, including MacArthur, considered to be no match for American Soldiers and Marines. His decision to push his forces north to the Yalu River was premised on a major false assumption: that China lacked the political and military will to intervene in the conflict.[187] Along with other American officials, MacArthur believed that the Chinese communists feared the consequences of war with the United States and would not intervene overtly on behalf of North Korea.[188] MacArthur's total underestimation of the Chinese military was shared by some of his subordinates, such as Major General Ned Almond, commander of X Corps, who stated emphatically to his subordinate commanders, "We're still attacking and we're going all the way to the Yalu. Don't let a bunch of Chinese laundrymen stop you."[189] In light of ample evidence to the contrary, which included the capture of Chinese prisoners of war in North Korea in late October and major action between US and Chinese forces in early November, MacArthur and other US strategic decision makers simply did not believe that the Chinese would dare to challenge the United States in Korea.[190] Described by Max Hastings as "one of the greatest and most persistent enigmas of the Korean War," this stubborn conviction by MacArthur and others that UN forces could cross deep into North Korea to China's border at the Yalu River without any punitive response or countermeasure by China's government was one of the most costly strategic oversights of the war for US forces.[191]

Despite the UNC's convictions to the contrary, China was indeed planning a major military intervention into the war. Mao Zedong, the Chairman of the Chinese Communist Party (CCP) and the head of state of the newly formed People's Republic of China, was not intimidated by the United States'

---

[187] Stanlis D. Milkowski, "After Inch'on: MacArthur's 1950 Campaign in North Korea," *Historical Perspectives of the Operational Art,* Michael D. Krause and R. Cody Phillips, eds., (Washington: Center of Military History, 2007), 424.

[188] Shu Guang Zhang, *Mao's Military Romanticism: China and the Korean War, 1950-1953.* (Lawrence: University Press of Kansas, 1995), 85.

[189] Stewart, 4.

[190] Edwin P. Hoyt, *On to the Yalu,* (New York: Military Heritage Press, 1984), 252.

[191] Hastings, 129.

superiority in firepower and technology and was anxious to put a stop to US interference in China's sphere of influence.[192] The planning within the Chinese government for military involvement in the conflict began as early as 4 August 1950, when Mao called a Politburo meeting to discuss how and under what circumstances the PLA would intervene.[193] On 1 October he released a public statement saying, "The Chinese people will not tolerate foreign aggression and will not stand aside if the imperialists wantonly invade the territory of their neighbor."[194] Communications between Beijing and the Kremlin regarding Chinese plans for intervention were tense and uncertain. At the urging of Stalin and after several days of intense discussion at the top Chinese leadership, Mao decided to send the Chinese People's Volunteers to the war. His primary request to Stalin was for Soviet air support.[195] By 12 October, Mao had come to the conclusion that China would enter the war regardless of assistance from the Soviet Union. In a message to Zhou Enlai, who had flown to Moscow to seek Soviet military support, Mao stated that because American aggression in North Korea directly threatened the region's security, the Politburo had come to the unanimous decision that China would intervene with or without Soviet assistance.[196] Impressed with China's conviction, Stalin agreed to provide munitions, aircraft, and supplies for China's intervention.

Planning continued as China observed the NKPA's poor response to the UNC's landings at Inchon, the loss of Seoul to UNC forces, and the continuing UN offensive in September and early October. Finally, on 25 October the Chinese government announced that it would deploy the CPV to the Korean peninsula in order to "resist America, aid Korea, defend the country, and safeguard the home."[197]

---

[192] Shu Guang Zhang, 85.

[193] Xiaobing Li, 82.

[194] Fehrenbach, 187.

[195] Shu Guan Zhang, 83.

[196] *Ibid*, 84.

[197] Xiaobing Li, 79.

By this time hundreds of thousands of disciplined Chinese troops had already crossed the Yalu into North Korea in a massive covert operation and were concealed in the mountainous regions of North Korea south of the Yalu.[198]

The CPV was composed of the best units in the People's Liberation Army and drew its leadership and many of its troops from the Fourth and Third Field Armies, which were considered the finest and most experienced of the five field armies in the PLA.[199] The total Chinese force that intervened in Korea numbered some 300,000 soldiers organized into thirty divisions.[200] The field commanders of this force shared Mao Zedong's optimism and confidence that they could defeat the UNC. Having most recently triumphed in the Chinese Civil War against the "US trained and equipped" Guomindang Army, Peng Dehuai, the commander of Chinese forces in Korea, and his subordinates were anxious to check the "arrogance" of the United States and test their force against a major Western power.[201] Peng understood that many of the tactics that his army used so well in the civil war would not work in foreign soil against a well-armed and technologically advanced army, such as that of the United States in Korea. When his force crossed the Yalu, they carried with them the same mixed assortment of arms that they used at the end of the civil war.[202] Perhaps the greatest shortfall of the CPV was its highly antiquated logistical systems. The Chinese trickled supplies into Korea on the backs of soldiers at a laboriously slow rate. The system of gaining arms and supplies from adversaries that the Red Army employed well during the

---

[198] Hammel, 4.

[199] George, 6.

[200] *Ibid*, 6.

[201] Shu Guang Zhang, 85. It was long assumed that Lin Biao was the commander of the People's Volunteer Forces in Korea. Records reveal, however, that Lin Biao may have never participated in the Korean campaigns at all. The actual commander was Marshal Peng Dehuai, one of Mao's most important lieutenants and a hero of the Chinese civil war. See Harlan W. Jencks, *From Muskets to Missiles: Politics and Professionalism in the Chinese Army, 1945-1981,* (Boulder: Westview Press, 1982), 47.

[202] Jencks, 47.

civil war simply would not work in Korea against the US.[203] It was not until mid-1951 when the Soviet promise for air support and equipment finally began to materialize that this army would have the weaponry required to fight against a modern adversary. Until then the army would make do with what limited weapons and ammunition it had at a terrible expense in human lives during its First and Second Phase Offensives of 1950.

C. The Campaigns

After the completion of MacArthur's masterful envelopment in September, which included the X Corp's landings at Inchon and the Eighth Army's counteroffensive from Pusan, conditions were set for a final strike against the retreating North Korean forces. From Inchon, X Corps retook Seoul and days later conducted a link-up with lead elements of the Eighth Army near the capitol. The next phase of the operation was to capture Pyongyang. Against Walker's objections, the UNC plan was to attack Pyongyang from Wonsan on the east coast with X Corps while Eighth Army continued north, effectively blocking the withdrawal of North Korean forces in a second envelopment.[204] After the capture of Seoul, X Corps forces moved back to Inchon, loaded onto boats once again, circumnavigated the peninsula, and conducted an amphibious landing through the mine-filled harbor at Wonsan. This second major amphibious operation deeply complicated logistics, causing confusion and supply shortfalls.[205] Before the X Corps landed at Wonsan were complete, ROK forces had already pressed north and taken the city, thereby negating the purpose of the amphibious landing. The Eighth Army also continued its offensive northward, crossing the 38th parallel and advancing from Seoul to recapture Pyongyang by land.

---

[203] *Ibid.*

[204] Milkowski, 424.

[205] Stewart, 2.

By 19 October 1950 the UNC was nearing a decisive victory in North Korea.[206] The NKPA was disorganized and in retreat. UNC forces had seized Seoul, Pyongyang, and other major strategic objectives in the north. All that remained was the final defeat of the NKPA and the negotiations for a cease-fire and the major military actions of the war would be over. Therefore, MacArthur modified his instructions and ordered the Eighth Army and X Corps to rapidly drive forward via two axes towards the Yalu River, the border between China and North Korea.[207] Thus began the "race to the Yalu." The separate avenues of approach split the force, with Eighth Army in the west separated from X Corps on the eastern axis by the central spine of the North Korean mountains. In the drive northward, these two major maneuver elements were unable to mutually support the other due to the vast, rugged terrain between them. The X Corps was precipitously spread thin along many hundred miles of mountainous territory.

1. First Phase Offensive

Despite sufficient evidence by late October that indicated the presence of major Chinese military forces in North Korea and the hardening resolve by the Chinese government to intervene militarily, MacArthur continued with his offensives beyond Pyongyang to the Yalu River.[208] The Chinese, who had been preparing their counterattack in great detail, planned to take full advantage of the American overconfidence and bravado by launching a massive surprise offensive.[209] When Mao ordered the Chinese People's Volunteers into North Korea on 19 October his instruction was to conduct the crossing and initiate operations covertly. "[The CPV] will first obtain a firm foothold in the areas in North Korea not yet lost to the enemy," he ordered, "then look for opportunities to fight a few battles of mobile

---

[206] Fehrenbach,

[207] Milkowski, 424.

[208] *Ibid*, 426.

[209] Shu Guan Zhang, 111.

warfare."[210] Taking this guidance, Peng's strategy was to fight a "combined positional and mobile warfare," in which "[the CPV will] firmly resist the enemy advance so as to keep it from forwarding even one more step; meanwhile, we will make a quick decision to strike out by penetrating into the enemy's rear wherever there is a weak point… Our present task," he explained to his subordinate commanders, "is to preserve a base, but more importantly, is to annihilate the enemy's strength. Therefore our defense is not completely defensive. It should enable us not only to eliminate the enemy but also to defend our positions."[211]

At 1730 on 19 October 1950, the first major wave of CPV soldiers began covertly crossing the Yalu into North Korea.[212] This initial wave consisted of 230,000 men in four armies.[213] By early November another 150,000 Chinese troops would be in North Korea, totaling thirty-three divisions and nearly half a million soldiers, which was approximately one tenth of the total forces of the PLA at the time.[214] Chinese strategic leadership believed that a massive deployment of troops would be needed to offset the UNC's superiority in firepower and technology.[215] The covert movement of so many Chinese forces across a major linear obstacle, the Yalu River, and over many hundreds of miles of mountainous terrain was an incredible feat that Hastings called "an extraordinary achievement of modern warfare."[216] Moving without the use of modern radios or mechanized equipment, hundreds of thousands of Chinese troops crossed deep into North Korea undetected, despite the UN's better technology and air superiority.

---

[210] Shu Guang Zhang, 93.

[211] *Ibid*, 89.

[212] Xiaobing Li, 86.

[213] The Chinese term "army" is roughly equivalent to a U.S. corps. CPV armies contained three divisions of approximately 10,000 men each. See Fehrenbach, 193.

[214] Xiaobing Li, 86.

[215] *Ibid*.

[216] Hastings, 137.

The first part of the offensive involved a large probing operation, in which the CPV conducted a series of limited attacks to determine the enemy strength, composition, and capabilities.[217] The purpose of these probes was also to test Chinese tactics against the well equipped US and UN coalition. These actions would provide Peng Dehuai the critical intelligence he needed to modify his operational design for the main offensive. The CPV fired their first shot against South Korean troops in Onjong in the early morning of 25 October. Using the heavy morning fog as concealment, Chinese forces surprised elements from the ROK 1st Division and destroyed a ROK battalion.[218] Fighting between the CPV and ROK forces continued throughout the last week of October the first week of November as large CPV units attacked numerous objectives throughout North Korea. Caught unprepared for a counteroffensive of this magnitude, ROK and US forces scrambled to establish defensive positions strung out across the country.[219]

However, by 6 November, CPV units began withdrawing from the front, breaking off action against UN forces and moving north. US commanders, including MacArthur, believed that the Communists had reached the end of their capabilities and no longer had the ability or will to sustain the offensive.[220] Peng, however, had a much different intention in mind with this operational pause. He directed each of his armies to give the impression that "we are being intimidated to retreat," and ordered the release of captured US and ROK troops to convey that message to their commanders.[221] Peng's strategy was to "encourage the enemy's arrogance" and to give them the impression that they had successfully fought off the Chinese intervention.[222] To "hook a big fish," he claimed, "you must let the

---

[217] Hammel, 5.

[218] Shu Guang Zhang, 102.

[219] Hammel, 5.

[220] Hastings, 138.

[221] Shu Guang Zhang, 110.

[222] Hastings, 138.

fish taste your bait. MacArthur boasts that he has never been defeated. We'll see who is going to wipe out whom!"[223] The sudden withdrawal of hundreds of thousands of Chinese troops succeeded in giving the UNC the illusion of victory, and MacArthur's confident thrust to the Yalu continued at full force on 25 November.[224] This deception concluded the Chinese First Phase Offensive, which would be followed by a massive attack across the entire front, called the Second Phase Offensive.

2. Second Phase Offensive

By 11 November 1950, the CPV Ninth Army, composing the second wave of the offensive, completed its crossing of the Yalu to reinforce Chinese forces in North Korea and prepare for a massive surprise attack on UN forces. By this time Peng had 230,000 troops in the west against 130,000 UN troops and 150,000 in the east against 90,000 UN troops.[225] His plan was to conduct a sequential attack on the UNC beginning with an assault against the US Eighth Army forces in the west with three army groups, the Thirty-Eighth, Forty-Second, and Fortieth Armies, and followed two days later by an attack against the US X Corps in the east with the Ninth Army.[226] [See Appendix 4, Figure 8C] On 25 November, Chinese forces began the surprise attack in the west against the U.S. IX Corps, the lead element of the Eighth Army. In this assault, the Chinese Thirty-Eighth and Forty-Second Armies attacked to destroy the ROK positions held by the ROK 7th and 8th Divisions and to penetrate the U.S. 2nd Infantry and 1st Cavalry Divisions.[227]

After two days of intense fighting, the Eighth Army was in immediate danger of being cut off from the south, forcing LTG Walker to order a withdrawal of his forces southwards. As the Eighth Army

---

[223] Shu Guang Zhang, 110.

[224] Hammel, 6.

[225] Xiaobing Li, 96.

[226] Shu Guang Zhang, 112-113.

[227] *Ibid,* 113.

began its retreat, Peng's intent was to inflict as much damage as possible on the fleeing UNC, choke its avenue of retreat, and strike a decisive blow on its main body.[228] The retreat for the Eighth Army was incredibly costly and a sense of fear and desperation began to grow in the Allied lines as repeated Chinese assaults pounded into the retreating columns of US and UN forces. By 6 December, the Eighth Army had withdrawn south of Pyongyang, giving up the North Korean capital to the CPV and was continuing to move southwards toward the 38th Parallel.

On the eastern front, the 150,000 Chinese troops from the Ninth Army Group launched their attack on 27 November against US forces centered at the Chosin Reservoir. [See Appendix 4, Figure 8D] Catching the U.S. 1st Marine and 7th Infantry Divisions by surprise, the CPV Ninth Army attacked with eight infantry divisions with disastrous effect on the UN position in the east.[229] The three divisions of the ROK II Corps had nearly collapsed in the attack and an eighty-mile gap separated the X Corps and the Eighth Army, preventing any mutual support between the eastern and western fronts.[230] The situation was worsening for US and ROK forces strung out across the vicinity of the Chosin Reservoir. The CPV Ninth Army attack separated the 1st Marine and 7th Infantry Divisions and surrounded them, pinning the 1st Marine Division at Hagaru-ri and the 7th Infantry Division at Chinhung-ri.[231] As Chinese forces bore down on his corps on 28 November, the commander of X Corps, MG Almond, flew to Tokyo to seek GEN MacArthur's guidance.[232] He returned to the battlefield the following day to issue the order for the "discontinuance of X Corp's attack to the northeast" and the general retreat and consolidation of his corps in the south.[233] That day, the Marines began a counterattack to break the Chinese encirclement and unite

---

[228] Shu Guang Zhang, 113.

[229] Xiaobing Li, 98.

[230] Hastings, 141.

[231] Xiaobing Li, 98.

[232] Stewart, 5.

[233] Ibid.

the scattered US forces in three isolated perimeters at Yudam-ni, Hagaru, and Koto-ri. The Battle of Chosin Reservoir continued for several days with intense fighting on both sides and massive casualties for both X Corps and the CPV Ninth Army, who were locked in combat that Fehrenbach described as "some of the most savage actions in the long history of land warfare."[234]

At Chosin, 25,000 X Corps troops were surrounded by the Ninth Army in the unforgiving, icy North Korean winter and the harsh rugged terrain of the Rangrim Mountains. Temperatures on the front reached as low as thirty degrees (F) below zero, as ice, snow, and bitter cold adversely affected Chinese and UN forces alike. The anchor of the Corps' defenses at the Chosin Reservoir was at Hagaru-ri, and by 31 November, Almond ordered his forces to retreat south of that location to Koto-ri, where the Corps would consolidate, reorganize, and continue movement to Hungnam. From this port city, the UNC could evacuate all friendly forces and many thousands of North Korean civilians by sea and air. Using the 3rd Infantry Division to cover the Corps' withdrawal, X Corps began its breakout from the Reservoir and the long march to the sea. On 1 December the Marines at Yudam-ni in the north of the Reservoir broke out of their encirclement, withdrawing under intense fire south to Hagaru-ri. An incredible assortment of UN air power covered X Corps' withdrawal from Hagaru-ri to Koto-ri as every bomber and attack aircraft in the Pacific was ordered to support the movement. By 7 December, UN forces had retreated south of Hagaru-ri continuously under Chinese fire along the "Hell Fire Valley" and the narrow mountain defiles leading out of the Reservoir.[235]

Fighting on the eastern front took an incredible toll on both sides. Despite many tactical successes, Chinese forces' employment of mobile warfare had thinly stretched the CPV's supply lines across North Korea. As UNC forces dug in against the Chinese onslaught, they brought to bear their vast

---

[234] Fehrenbach, 237 and Xiaobing Li. 98.

[235] Dvorchak, 135-136.

superiority in firepower and air power, relentlessly pounding Chinese lines.[236] The CPV Ninth Army lost nearly 40,000 men in the three weeks of fighting, rendering three divisions combat ineffective.[237] By 12 December, the 1st Marine Division successfully linked up with the 3rd Infantry Division at Hamhung and continued its movement to the ports at Hungnam.[238] From 10 to 24 December over 100,000 UN and ROK troops and 350,000 tons of equipment converged on Hungnam to conduct one of the largest evacuations in U.S. military history.[239] By 24 December, the final Allied battalions evacuated from the Hungnam perimeter, completing the X Corps strategic withdrawal from North Korea.

Ultimately, the CPV's First and Second Phase Offensives were a strategically successful campaign, albeit a rather pyrrhic victory. Suffering more than 80,000 casualties on both fronts of the operation, Chinese forces were able to achieve Mao's strategic objectives of the Chinese intervention in North Korea, but at a great cost in lives and materiel.[240] Mao Zedong's own family suffered loss in this campaign, as Mao's eldest living son, Mao Anying, was killed by a UNC airstrike on 27 November.[241] The campaign took a great toll on United Nations Forces lives as well. On both fronts, an estimated 15,000 UN casualties resulted from the fighting, including the death of the Eighth Army Commander, LTG Walker, by a vehicular accident on 23 December 1950.[242] The campaign successfully pushed UN forces out of North Korea below the 38th Parallel and enabled the recapture of Pyongyang. It checked American "arrogance" and tested the capabilities of the Chinese military for the first time against a major

---

[236] Jencks, 47.

[237] Xiaobing Li, 99.

[238] Robert J. Dvorchak, *Battle for Korea: A History of the Korean Conflict,* (Pennsylvania: The Associated Press, 1993), 135.

[239] Stewart, 21-23.

[240] Xiaobing Li, 100.

[241] Not surprisingly, Mao Zedong was not notified of his son's death until a month after the event. Fearing his leader's reaction, Peng Dehuai withheld the news and waited several weeks before relaying the incident through Zhou Enlai, the Vice Chairman of the CCP Military Commission and Premier of the PRC.

[242] Center for Military History, *The Chinese Intervention: 3 November 1950-24 January 1951,* (CMH Publication 19-8) http://www.history.army.mil/brochures/kw-chinter/chinter.htm, (accessed 15 April 2010).

Western power. This massive Chinese intervention turned the tide of the war, saving the North Korean government and army from the brink of destruction. It set the conditions for the Third Phase Offensive, which would push UNC forces below the 37th Parallel and enable the recapture of the South Korean capitol at Seoul.

C. Analysis

1. Orientation at the Strategic Level of War

Mao Zedong understood the importance of achieving one's strategic political goals when designing military campaigns. During the Chinese Civil War he developed his strategic orientation and used that focus to great advantage against the GMD. Extending this principle to the Korean War, Mao understood that the key to victory lay in the accomplishment of strategic tasks and the sequencing of tactical and operational activities towards strategic ends, not simply the achievement of individual victories at the tactical level. In his writings during the Civil War, he expounded his beliefs on effective strategy, which he termed the "study of the laws of a war situation as a whole." In his essay, *Strategy in China's Revolutionary War*, he wrote:

> In the history of war, there are instances where defeat in a single battle nullified all of the advantages of a series of victories, and there are also instances where victory in a single battle after many defeats opened up a new situation. In those instances the 'series of victories' and the 'many defeats' were partial in nature and not decisive for the situation as a whole, while 'defeat in a single battle or 'victory in a single battle' played the decisive role. All this explains the importance of taking into account the situation as a whole.[243]

To accomplish strategic objectives, Mao understood that he and his operational commander, Peng, had to focus on strategic objectives and endstates, giving primary consideration to the relation between the enemy and themselves, the relation between various campaigns and stages of the war, the

---

[243] Mao Zedong, "Strategy in China's Revolutionary War," *Selected Writings of Mao Zedong*, Combat Studies Institute ed., 81-82.

accomplishment of decisive operations, and the sequencing of their forces in time, space, and activity.[244] Important to both Mao and Peng was ensuring that all activity was nested with a broad operational approach that focused on the achievement of strategic objectives. Mao's announcement to the Chinese people on 25 October explained that the purpose of intervention in Korea was to "resist America, aid Korea, defend the country, and safeguard the home."[245] In a dispatch to Moscow on 2 October, Mao described his strategic objectives in North Korea. "We shall aim at resolving the conflict, that is, to eliminate the U.S. troops within Korea or to drive them and other countries' aggressive forces out of [North Korea]." His second strategic objective was to "bring out a successful resolution of the Korean conflict" without America declaring a general war on China and attacking its territory.[246]

Before deploying the CPV into North Korea the Chinese high command developed these broad goals into more focused strategic objectives for the First and Second Phase Offensives. Understanding the will and intent of his political leadership, Peng designed campaign objectives that would support the accomplishment of the state's political objectives. His overall strategy was to fight "a combined positional and mobile warfare" that would enable the CPV to achieve three critical operational objectives. First, the CPV would conduct a covert infiltration into North Korea and "extend and consolidate a foothold in the mountainous areas north of the line between Wonsan and Pyongyang."[247] Accomplishing this would set the conditions for the next operational objective, which Peng described as "luring the enemy forces into our internal line and wiping them out one by one."[248] The final operational objective of the campaign was to launch a major attack on the U.S. Eighth Army and X Corps forces in North

---

[244] Mao Zedong, "Strategy in China's Revolutionary War," 83-84.

[245] Xiaobing Li, 79.

[246] Shu Guang Zhang, 78.

[247] *Ibid*, 99.

[248] *Ibid*, 109.

Korea to "surround and annihilate one [enemy column]."[249] This would support strategic endstates because Peng believed that "if [the CPV] can annihilate two or three U.S. and ROK divisions, the Korean war would fundamentally turn in [its] favor."

By achieving these operational objectives, the CPV would be able to meet Mao's strategy of decisively repelling US forces from North Korea and if executed correctly would prevent China from being entangled in an operational stalemate against the UNC in North Korea while US forces declared war on and attacked the Chinese mainland. Having worked closely alongside Mao since the Long March in 1934, Peng intuitively understood his Chairman's strategic intentions and focused his operational design to achieve the political goals of the war.   Unlike MacArthur, whose operational approach after Inchon and "race to the Yalu" seriously risked major strategic ramifications, such as sparking a general war between the U.S. and China or the U.S.S.R., Peng's campaign plan was designed to achieve strategic endstates and was oriented at the strategic level of war. MacArthur's focus on the tactical task of decisively and rapidly destroying the NKPA caused him to deeply overextend his forces and brought on an undesirable strategic escalation of the war. Peng's focus on the strategic task of forcing the UNC out of North Korea, enabled him to fight a successful campaign that was nested with the political will of his state's leadership.

2. Strategic Maneuver

Many American accounts of combat against Chinese forces in 1950 suggested that China's strategy was centered on attritional warfare. The Chinese approach, according to these accounts, was to use its manpower superiority to overwhelm the UNC with "human wave" or "Chinese horde" attacks, during which CPV units would mindlessly assault with wave after wave of soldiers, regardless of the cost in human lives. If these accounts were correct, it would suggest that Chinese forces in Korea had

---

[249] Shu Guang Zhang, 108.

80

diverged from principles established during the Chinese Civil War, such as the preservation of forces, strategic maneuver, and deception operations required of Mao Zedong's theory of mobile warfare. While this may have seemed the case for news media on the battlefields of North Korea, the after action reviews of American combat units provide a better military assessment of Chinese strategy and tactics in the Korean War.[250] The official U.S. Marine Corps history of the Korean War gives an excellent insight into how the Chinese actually fought in 1950:

> Press correspondents were found of referring to 'the human sea tactics of the Asiatic hordes.' Nothing could be further from the truth. In reality the Chinese seldom attacked in units larger than a regiment. Even these efforts were usually reduced to a seemingly endless succession of platoon infiltrations. It was not mass but deception and surprise which made the Chinese Red formidable…[CPV] advancing columns took such natural routes as draws or stream beds, deploying as soon as they came into resistance. Combat groups then peeled off from the tactical columns, one at a time, and closed with rifles, submachine guns, and grenades…When fully committed they did not relinquish the attack even when riddled with casualties. Other Chinese came forward to take their places, and the build-up continued until a penetration was made, usually on the front of one or two platoons…Each step of the assault was executed with practiced stealth and boldness, and the results of such penetrations on a battalion front could be devastating.[251]

Described in this account is not attritional warfare, as may have been suggested by media and other non-military accounts of the war, but mobile warfare, waged by a determined force that took advantage of relative force ratios and maneuver to achieve positional advantages against its enemy. While Chinese attacks sustained incredible casualty rates, they were purposeful and were focused to achieve a tactical or operational advantage. These methods of attack were not designed simply to overcome the enemy's position with superior numbers but to exploit weakness his lines and to dominate him where he is disadvantaged. The operational maneuver and battlefield tactics employed by the CPV were not human wave assaults but well orchestrated *forms of maneuver*, specifically infiltrations and

---

[250] George, 3.

[251] *Ibid*, 3-4.

penetrations.[252]   The assessment made in this Marine Corps account was that when the Chinese relentlessly massed forces it was to achieve penetrations of UNC lines and defensive positions.

The success of the CPV against UNC forces during these two offensives was due in large part to the successful execution of strategic maneuver in accordance with Mao's precepts on mobile warfare and adapted for warfare against the US military in North Korean terrain. When analyzed at the operational level of war, the CPV offensives in 1950 may be divided into four discernable stages of maneuver: infiltration, penetration, exploitation, and pursuit. The CPV's operational infiltration occurred from October to November 1950 when Chinese forces successfully and covertly crossed the Yalu River with five field armies without being detected by UNC surveillance. Once these forces were in place, the CPV massed forces at decisive points of penetration to breech X Corps' wide and exposed front in the east and disrupt Eighth Army's still approaching and dispersed column in the west.

Once they had surprised UN forces and successfully penetrated UNC lines, Chinese forces seized the initiative and continued the offensive with a major exploitation attack on both fronts. The major attacks against the Eighth Army at the Ch'ongch'on River and the X Corps at Chosin were part of this exploitation attack. Finally, the CPV attempted, but were unsuccessful in the final phase of the offensive, pursuit. This phase of the operation failed because of the UNC's successful employment of massive airpower and artillery in support of troops withdrawing to Hungnam in the east and the 38th Parallel in the west. Therefore, the Chinese First and Second Phase Offensive were not an attrition-based campaign, as suggested by some accounts of the Korean War, but one founded on sound maneuver warfare principles and designed to exploit the CPV's superiority in numbers and nullify the UNC's materiel advantages.

----

[252] The U.S. Army's *Field Manual 3-90: Tactics* describes five forms of maneuver: envelopment, turning movement, infiltration, penetration, and frontal attack. An infiltration is "a form of maneuver in which an attacking force conducts undetected movement through or into an area occupied by enemy forces to occupy a position of advantage in the enemy rear while exposing only small elements to enemy defensive fires." A penetration is "a form of maneuver in which an attacking force seeks to rupture enemy defenses on a narrow front to disrupt the defensive system." See Headquarters, Department of the Army, *Field Manual 3-90: Tactics,* (Washington: July 2001), pages 3-11, 3-19, and 3-25.

3. Shaping Operations

Shaping operations were critical to the successful execution of the CPV's offensive in 1950. Several Chinese field army commanders favored a Chinese military intervention in Korea, should North Korea be threatened and had agreed in a meeting in August 1950 that the best time for the Chinese to attack would be after the UNC crossed the 38th Parallel but before they could consolidate and reorganize their gains in North Korea.[253] The Chinese high command believed that this and other key conditions must be set before launching the main attack against the UNC. Understanding the critical importance of shaping operations to shift the probability of success in one's favor, Peng designed a sequential campaign in phases. Each phase set the conditions for the initiation of the next and contributed to the overall favorable outcome of the campaign.

Five phases may be discerned from the conduct of this operation on the Chinese side. The first phase was the covert infiltration of the CPV from Manchuria into North Korea in two waves from October to November of 1950. Peng and his subordinate commanders understood the critical importance of moving the force and concealing it well within North Korea intact and undetected. If the infiltration was compromised, Chinese forces would become vulnerable to UNC airpower and the UNC would alter its maneuver plan to better prepare for major combat operations against a large force north of Pyongyang. This would rob the Chinese of the initiative, disrupt their movement south, and make the main attack across both fronts more difficult and costly. Therefore, deception and stealth were the key conditions of the first phase that would enable the second, which was the probing operation conducted in early November 1950. In this phase, the CPV gained critical intelligence of the enemy disposition, composition, and strength, which enabled Peng and his army commanders to determine weaknesses to

---

[253] Shu Guang Zhang, 75.

exploit in the main attack and allowed the CPV to test their own tactics and assess their enemy's capabilities. This phase would close the CPV's intelligence gaps and enable a refinement of the plan.

Once the conditions of this phase were set, the CPV could continue with the next, which involved the operational withdrawal north to "bait" the UNC into the main Chinese attack. Finally, once the UNC continued north and was convinced that the Chinese did not have the will to fight a major engagement, the CPV could launch its final phase, the near simultaneous two-front assault against the U.S. Eighth Army in the west and the X Corps in the east. Each of these critical shaping operations set the conditions for success in the subsequent phase and contributed to the overall accomplishment of the campaign plan. Peng's understanding of shaping operations was evident in the great care and effort put into each phase to facilitate the conduct of the decisive operation, the main attack. Fully understanding how to use shaping operations to arrange the conditions of the campaign in its favor, the CPV was able to nullify or reduce many of the advantages enjoyed by the UNC, such as superior firepower and combined arms capabilities, at the decisive time and place in the campaign for the Chinese.

4. Deception

Deception was a key element in the operational plan of the First and Second Phase Offensives. Mao Zedong and Peng Dehuai understood well that their army, though sizeable and experienced, could not match the military technology and firepower of the UNC. The CPV lacked sufficient airpower, precision artillery, and advanced small arms necessary to match the UNC's weaponry and equipment. However, both Mao and Peng were no strangers to fighting against a technologically superior and more lethally armed adversary. During their campaigns during most of the Chinese Civil War, the Communist Red Army, commanded by Mao and led operationally by field commanders like Peng, incorporated strategies, such as the use of unorthodox warfare and deception, that helped to negate the GMD's materiel advantages. They understood the decisive advantage provided by the element of surprise and designed their campaign so that they could catch the UNC unprepared to defend against a major offensive.

An important element in the use of deception in combat is to understand one's enemy and exploit that knowledge to achieve surprise. While Mao and Peng deeply understood the qualities, capabilities, and intentions of their adversary, the operational leadership of UN forces failed to understand the Chinese. Despite radio broadcasts of Chinese intent, the confirmed movements of large Chinese units in Manchuria, and tactical intelligence that proved that Chinese military forces were already in North Korea, MacArthur had already made up his mind about the potential for Chinese intervention, which he was convinced was merely a bluff.[254] Whether convinced by the assessment of his GHQ intelligence officer, Major General Charles Willoughby, and many others of the unwillingness of the Chinese political authority to intervene, or as some have suggested, "intoxicated with the heady taste of triumph," MacArthur simply convinced himself early on that the Chinese were not a threat.[255] Even if Chinese forces lay between the UNC and the Yalu River, MacArthur believed that his airpower could destroy them if they tried to intervene. Likewise, his commanders, as Max Hastings suggested, were "blinded to what was taking place on [their front]…They had persuaded themselves that the war was all but over. Their senses were deadened to any fresh perception."[256]

Recognizing their enemy's overconfidence and lack of understanding, Mao and Peng designed the first phase of the operation to be a major covert operation. Deception was key to achieving operational surprise and catching the UNC unprepared and vulnerable. This massive surprise attack would offset the UNC's superiority in firepower and materiel, put it in a mode of reaction rather than action, and seize and maintain the initiative for the Chinese. The importance of deception to this operation was evident in the extraordinary care that the CPV took in making the movement of hundreds of thousands of troops and equipment in six field armies across the Yalu River and into the mountains of North Korea. This secret deployment of ground forces was a remarkable feat, requiring the utmost

---

[254] Fehrenbach, 189.

[255] *Ibid*, 189.

[256] Hastings, 137.

discipline across the ranks of the army, exceptional tactical fieldcraft, night movement expertise, and the skillful use of cover and concealment throughout many miles of difficult, mountainous terrain. Ultimately, the CPV's deception worked as intended, giving the Chinese not only the element of surprise but decisive positional advantages and the initiative over the United Nations Command.

D. Conclusion

The First and Second Phase Offensives provide an exceptional glimpse into the evolution and conduct of Chinese warfare in the modern day. Although the Chinese people paid a heavy price in human lives during this military intervention in the Korean War, the campaign achieved all of its strategic objectives and sent a clear message to the United Nations and the world that the People's Republic of China, though newly formed, had the capability and will to protect its regional interests and assert its military power in East Asia. These offensives were the PLA's first true military challenge against a powerful Western adversary, forcing it to quickly modify its Civil War organization, military strategies, and tactics to survive and win major combat operations in Korea. While it suffered from materiel deficiencies, antiquated logistical systems, and inefficient command and control, the CPV benefited greatly from its application of the methods and propensities of the Chinese way of war.

Mao Zedong, who deeply understood the philosophy of the ancient classic Chinese strategists, learned to adapt this learning to modern military operations during the Chinese Civil War. Following in this tradition, the operation's commander, Peng was also able to successfully apply traditional Chinese warfighting strategies to achieve success during his campaigns in North Korea. This operation clearly reveals the continuities in the propensities of Chinese warfare from the medieval era to the present and shows how ancient warfighting strategies, when modified for the contemporary operational environment and applied correctly, can contribute to victory on the modern battlefield. This campaign demonstrates that the Chinese way of war continues to exist and maintain relevancy in the modern era.

VII. Conclusion

The purpose of this research was to analyze Chinese military history throughout different periods to reveal the trends and continuities of Chinese warfare and to determine if a Chinese way of war exists. In this analysis we see that warfare in China has evolved considerably throughout the last two thousand years, and the long military history of this civilization is colorful, varied, and distinctive. Yet despite its dynamic evolution, there are four propensities of Chinese warfighting, which are rooted in ancient Chinese military philosophy, that recur and echo across many centuries of warfare in China. When one broadly considers the China's long military history, the four propensities emerge to form a unique Chinese way of war. These propensities provide continuities between the traditions of the armies of ancient China and its modern day military forces and make Chinese warfighting distinctive from that of other civilizations. This Chinese way of war is a product of China's unique cultural traditions, religious and social philosophies, and historical evolution.

A deep understanding of Chinese warfare is important today because of the global role that the People's Republic of China continues to play in contemporary international affairs. China has the largest military in the world and its focus has begun to shift from internal security and maintenance of its regional hegemony to protection and promotion of its strategic interests around the world. Studies of China's unique warfighting preferences and practices throughout history can help to bridge the gap of understanding in the West of how China wages war, its tendencies at the strategic and operational levels of war, and the military philosophies that underpin its warfighting strategies and orientations. As China assumes its role as a leading global power in the twenty-first century, it becomes increasingly important for the United States to understand and learn from Chinese military traditions and practices. It is certain that in this century, the governments, economies, and military forces of the United States and China will come into increasing contact. Whether this contact comes in the form of partnership and cooperation or adversarial activity, understanding of the Chinese way of war can help to better prepare the United States for its future interactions with the Chinese government and military.

The study of Chinese warfare in the U.S. Army's officer education system lacks depth and substance. The focus of the Army's military history programs from junior to mid-grade leader development courses lies almost exclusively in Western warfare. Absent in this education is any substantive analysis of China's military history or its unique philosophies of warfare. This educational shortcoming has contributed to a lack of understanding across the force about China, its military, and its martial traditions and practices. It is troubling that the study of warfare for American officers offers little or no inclusion of non-Western warfare. This deficiency must be corrected in order to create a new appreciation for Chinese military history and to gain a deeper understanding of non-Western ways in war. In addition to the study of Clausewitz, Jomini, Mahan, and other great Western military philosophers, U.S. military education programs should also provide analyses of Sunzi, Mao, and some of the other great Chinese strategists. Operational case studies should also be broadened to include some of the decisive wars, campaigns, and battles of modern Chinese history, which will provide a greater appreciation of non-Western warfare and give new insights into China's military practices.

Adjusting these education programs is an important step towards bridging the present gap in understanding of China and Chinese warfare in the U.S. military. Since the near future will most likely involve increased interaction and partnership between the militaries of the United States and China, it would be appropriate and prudent to broaden American officer education with greater emphasis on Chinese military history, philosophy, and culture. Greatly needed to enhance this program are more English language translations of Chinese military texts, histories, documents, and other sources relevant to any thorough study of warfare. Additionally, schools within the U.S. Army's Training and Doctrine Command should consider employing more Chinese military experts and other academic professionals to assist in balancing the curricula to include more substantive analysis of non-Western warfare.

The analysis provided in this monograph gives only a small glimpse into the history of Chinese warfare. While the three case studies of this research shed light on the military practices of their respective eras, the work skips many hundreds of years of Chinese military. To better develop the theory of the Chinese way of war, future research topics must fill in the substantial gaps left by this work. Areas for study include analyses of campaigns in the Warring States Period (475-221 BCE), during which many of the classic writings of Chinese military philosophy were written, warfare during the imperial dynasties of the Song (960-1297 CE), Yuan (1271–1368), Ming (1368–1644), and Qing Dynasties (1644-1911), and other campaigns of the modern era, including those of the Republic of China (1912-1949) and the People's Republic of China (1949 to the present).

A methodological problem that this study suffers from, which future research can work to correct, is its need to provide more substantive consideration of the foreign and domestic politics and other elements of the strategic environment that may have affected the outcome of the three campaigns studied. A greater analysis of the strategic considerations and geopolitical pressures of these campaigns may shed greater light on *why* the armies fought the way they did at the strategic level of war. Subsequent studies could also analyze in greater detail the cultural, religious, and social influences of the Chinese civilization that shaped its way of war. By analyzing the Chinese way of war from a broader perspective, future research could also help to prevent the historical fallacy of oversimplification, in which this work and several other "way of war" theories may err.

Political and military relations between the United States and China in the twenty-first century continue to change and evolve from the inconsistent and often strained patterns of the previous century. Yet globalization, modern communications technology, and international economics have brought these two powerful nations closer in partnership than ever before. As the U.S. and China become increasingly interdependent, the impetus and motivation to better understand each other grows. Regardless of whether the near future of these two global powers is friendly or adversarial, it is critically important for US military leaders and other strategic decision makers to better understand and appreciate Chinese strategic orientations, the propensities of its operational art, and its general philosophical views on warfare. The study of the Chinese way of war can help to illuminate these important topics and provide insight into the unique qualities, continuities, and traditions of Chinese warfare throughout history. To fully understand China, one must study its military history, which has so indelibly shaped the unique character and distinctive attributes of that extraordinary civilization.